Praise for *But I Didn't Say Goodbye*

"*But I Didn't Say Goodbye* is an inspiring chronicle of the five-year journey of an eleven-year-old suicide survivor. Barbara Rubel presents a powerful portrait of the myriad of thoughts and feelings so common to those of all ages after the death of a friend or family member by suicide. This story helps readers to normalize their grief and not feel isolated after this sudden and traumatic death. *But I Didn't Say Goodbye* also serves as a practice resource and tool to work with children and adults with the delicate and sensitive topic of suicide. It is an invaluable guide for all those facing the aftermath of suicide and an inspiration of hope for acceptance of one of life's most difficult challenges. I recommend it highly."

—Linda Goldman, author, *Life and Loss, Breaking the Silence, Bart Speaks Out, Raising Our Children to Be Resilient and Coming Out, Coming In*

"'Why do you push me aside?'", ask grieving adults. Kids ask (in their way), too! It is a sad way of life for many on their grief journey. When the loss is due to suicide, the grievers may feel pushed so far that they are off the planet. Even with all the efforts to educate, heighten awareness, and change attitudes, it still is common that the horrific sorrow of suicide grief is compounded, not comforted, by all too many. Barbara Rubel has given much of her professional life to the needs of the bereaved, especially those most marginalized. This book must be read, and read again, so that we can be messengers of hope to these grieving adults . . . and kids!"

—Rev. Richard B. Gilbert, PhD, CT, Faculty, Mercy College, Dobbs Ferry, NY, Benedictine University of Illinois and The Graduate Theological Foundation

"This book is accessible and useful both for suicide survivors and for those trying to help them through the experience. Children and others will readily relate to the narrator's personal experience. Professionals, parents, and others can use this book as a foundation and guide to supporting survivors of suicide on their path towards healing."

—Ricky Greenwald, PsyD, Founder/Director, Child Trauma Institute; author, *Child Trauma Handbook*

"Barbara Rubel has written a much needed fictional story that applies the thoughts, emotions, and experiences of a young boy who has lost his father to a suicide. Rubel takes the fictional family through the grieving process in a sensitive and compassionate way. This is an area which takes great courage to address and yet the most vulnerable of our society, our children are often left struggling to comprehend what has happened, and what has happened to them in terms of loss and grieving. I am delighted that Rubel has combined both fiction with hands on activities and questions to help foster discussion with children. I recommend this valuable book and resource to anyone—both professionals and families."

—Julia Sorensen, Therapist and author, *Overcoming Loss: Stories and Activities to Help Children Transform Grief and Loss,* Canada, www.thecbtcoach.com

"*But I Didn't Say Goodbye* is an easy-to-read guide which provides valuable insights and practical ideas for helping adolescents who have lost someone to suicide to regain control over devastating emotions."

—Bev Cobain, author, *When Nothing Matters Anymore: A Survival Guide for Depressed Teens,* and *Dying to Be Free: A Healing Guide for Families After a Suicide*

"I wish I'd had *But I Didn't Say Goodbye* when my brother, Bill, died by suicide 28 years ago. This book would have helped me through much of the pain in the days immediately following his death and prevented many of the missteps I took along the way. Barbara Rubel's deft handling of the many horrific facets of suicide loss was as artistic as it was powerful. The book's style and insight will bring families closer and help heal the heart of those who've lost—be they young or old. *But I Didn't Say Goodbye* beautifully weaves all of the emotion and terrifying issues a child faces when they've lost a parent to suicide, solidifying its place as an invaluable resource for survivors. While addressing the painful elements of the survivor's experience (fear, longing, guilt, stigma), Rubel also addresses the role of mental illness and the need for open, honest communication among the family. Use this book as a guide for your own healing the first time and as a source of solace every time thereafter."

—Mike Reynolds, author, *Surviving Bill*

"Barbara Rubel's, *But I Didn't Say Goodbye*, 2nd Edition, is an incredible resource written with compassion, empathy and insight. It is a comprehensive guide to utilize in addressing the many challenges facing survivors. Additionally, this book will empower professional caregivers in their work with those grieving a suicide."

—Doreen Cammarata MS, LMHC, author, *Someone I Love Died by Suicide: A Story for Child Survivors and Those Who Care for Them*

"For far too long suicide has remained in the closet. Throughout my career working with children and families, suicide was consistently the most difficult loss for families to cope with, oftentimes due to the secrecy imposed by parents who believed they were protecting their children from the pain the truth would cause. *But I Didn't Say Goodbye* is one of the few resources available to help children and families grieving due to the death of a loved one by suicide. Barbara Rubel has written a book that takes us along as the family struggles to heal after the suicide of the father. This book is an invaluable tool to assist children in understanding and working with their own feelings and experience, while also providing parents with a guideline for communicating with their children. I highly recommend this important resource."

—Virginia A. Simpson, Ph.D., FT, Founder, Executive Director & Program Director, The Mourning Star Center; Director of Grief Education, FuneralOne

"*But I Didn't Say Goodbye* is a wonderful book that stimulates both thoughts and feelings. The book is very well written and is a unique resource for adolescents and preadolescents if they experience a death by suicide. Reading this book will make an important contribution to their understanding. When young people experience a suicide in the family or another sudden death of a loved one, they often experience strange thoughts and more intense feelings than ever before. *But I Didn't Say Goodbye* represents a unique gift to them as it, in a concrete way, describes the questions they will have to deal with and the answers (and lack of answers) to be found. This book will help them integrate the past, increase their grip on the present, and make them hopeful for the future.

The author has, in a remarkable way, given them a map of the unknown terrain they will move in without providing easy solutions. The chapters or parts of the book can be read between sessions, discussed in individual sessions, or in grief groups. Parents and sensitive caretakers can also let this book be a starting point for their own conversations with a grieving teenager."

—Atle Dyregrov, PhD, Founder and Director, Center for Crisis Psychology, Bergen, Norway, author, *Grief in Children, Grief in Young Children*, and *Effective Grief and Bereavement Support*

"A richly imaginative and innovative work that is solidly grounded and eminently readable . . . An invaluable resource in the study of suicidology."

—Rabbi Earl Grollman, DHL, DD, (on the first edition), author with Max Malikow, *Living When a Young Friend Commits Suicide*

"SAVE applauds the honesty and accuracy of this book. At long last an author tells the truth to children about the cause of suicide. The words depression, disease and chemical imbalance in the brain are music to the ears of suicide prevention advocates working to erase centuries of ignorance."

—Mary Kluesner (on the first edition), President, SAVE, Suicide Awareness Voices of Education

"The heartbroken questing of Alex in *But I Didn't Say Goodbye* echo the few, the struggle to understand, the needed for reassurance and comfort by children bereaved by suicide everywhere. *But I Didn't Say Goodbye* responds to Alex's questions of suicide, confident of promoting the child's healthy grief resolution and laying a sound foundation for the child's future well-being."

—LaRita Archibald (on the first edition), *HEARTBEAT, Support in the Aftermath of Suicide*

"*But I Didn't Say Goodbye* is clearly outlined. It not only tells us who the book is for, but how they can use it. The author, Barbara Rubel, begins by telling her own story, the suicide of her father. The book is as much a need to educate us, as it is her need for healing. Of course, this is the key to any good survivors book in the field. What allows this book to resonate to us is the actual verbalizations of Alex, a young boy faced with the 'unfaceable'—his daddy's suicide. Barbara guides us through the questions, blames, issues . . . and PAIN of a young person. It does so through the actual protocols of Alex—of course, narrative accounts have always been richer than just words. Suicide notes are a good example. One can feel the boy's pain . . . the protocols do justice to the rich individuality of each of us, something that no statistical, scientific report can. It provides us with the ideographic approach that has been central to suicidology since Shneidman and Farberow's 1957 monumental book, *Clues to Suicide*.

Alex's protocols not only allow us to understand the young boy's aftershocks but also provide a guide for us to help—Alex's dialogues with his mother, uncle, grandparent, coach, show us direction. It shows a basic fact in postvention. Everyone can help in the healing process. Indeed, it takes the community to help our Alexs'. As a final guidance, Barbara Rubel in her book presents the ultimate healing to quote Alex's grandmother, 'I love you Alex.' Eros can do wonders in our life."

—Antoon A. Leenaars (on the first edition), *Psychotherapy, Consultation, Research and Specialized Workshops, Windsor, Ontario Canada*

"As someone who, as a child, lost his father to suicide, I warmly recommend Barbara Rubel's book. It will help suicide survivors deal with the bafflement, sense of abandonment, and depression that are so often the sad legacies of suicide. Rubel suggests how the child can discover some meaning in an act that often seems to erode meaning and value, and how the child can begin to cope with and surmount a tragedy that will, in some respects, be with him or her for a lifetime."

—Larry Lockridge (on the first edition), Professor of English, NY University, author, *Shade of the Raintree: The Life and Death of Ross Lockridge, Jr.*, author of Raintree County

But I Didn't Say Goodbye

Helping Children and Families
After a Suicide

Barbara Rubel

Second Edition

Griefwork Center, Inc.
New Jersey

AUTHOR'S NOTE
The author gives permission for exercises at the end of each chapter to
be copied and used freely by the reader in his or her practice setting.

Published by
Griefwork Center, Inc.
P.O. Box 5177
Kendall Park, NJ 08824
Orders: www.griefworkcenter.com

ISBN-13 978-1-892906-01-4
ISBN-10 1-892906-01-5

Printed in the United States of America

Library of Congress Control Number 2008910966

This publication is designed to present information in regard to the
subject matter covered. The author and publisher are not providing
psychological services. If professional counseling is needed, services of
a qualified professional should be sought. The author and Griefwork
Center, Inc. have neither liability nor responsibility to any individual
with regard to any loss or harm abused, or alleged to be caused directly
or indirectly, by the material in this book.

For my children
Alan, Matthew, Michael, and Brian.
When your grandfather died by suicide,
grief touched my heart.
When each of you were born,
my heart was filled with love.
Through the years, you have became my greatest teachers.
You taught me that bonds are never severed.
We live on through our memories.
Memories of my dad have become my sweetest stories.
If you are ever touched by grief,
share your memories and your stories
with those who fill your hearts with love.

—Mom

Contents

About the Author

Barbara Rubel, MA, BCETS, CBS, CPBC is a nationally recognized bereavement specialist and author of the 30-hour continuing education course book for Nurses, *Death, Dying, and Bereavement*, sold through Western Schools. Three weeks prior to giving birth to triplets, her father, a retired New York City Police Officer, died by suicide. Her story was featured in the Emmy award-winning documentary, *Fatal Mistakes: Families Shattered by Suicide*, narrated by Mariette Hartley. Barbara is a Consultant for the U.S. Department of Justice, Office for Victims of Crime (OVCTTAC). She is the co-author, with Angie McCown, of the OVC Compassion Fatigue curriculum. Barbara wrote a chapter, "A Doctor's Note," In H. Stone. (Ed.), *Remembering Our Angels* (pp. 12–23, 2007). She also created and developed The Palette of Grief® Program.

Barbara is a Board Certified Expert in Traumatic Stress and Diplomate, American Academy of Experts in Traumatic Stress. She is a Certified Bereavement Specialist, a Certified Pastoral Bereavement Counselor and is trained in Critical Incident Stress Management. Barbara received her BS in Psychology and MA in Community Health with a concentration in Thanatology from Brooklyn College.

Barbara was a Hospice Pastoral Bereavement Counselor and facilitated several support groups. In 1995, she created and facilitated the support group, *Sharing Our Loss After Suicide (SOLAS)*. She taught undergraduate and graduate courses at Brooklyn College including Crisis Intervention, Children and Death, and Health Counseling. Barbara served as a Consultant for the NJ Office of the Attorney General and UMDNJ to support those impacted by September 11.

Barbara Rubel is a member of the Association for Death, Education and Counseling; International Critical Incident Stress Foundation, Inc.; American Association of Suicidology; and the American Foundation for Suicide Prevention.

Acknowledgments

From the time I first decided to write *But I Didn't Say Goodbye*, through its drafts, I have been encouraged by many talented people. They were helpful in integral ways, reading this work in manuscript form, offering helpful, constructive comments, or giving examples from their personal experience. Virginia A. Simpson made many invaluable suggestions with respect to content and provided thoughtful reading on early drafts. Chimere Holmes and Sydne Matus offered helpful editorial comments. For his time and suggestions, I thank Leon Wollersheim. I am particularly appreciative of Susan Thomas, who provided insight about children bereavement support groups. Finally, I wish to acknowledge with sincere gratitude all my readers for their helpful comments, Bonnie Shields, Joyce Williams, Liz Powell, Toni Griffith, Joy Johnson, Laura Munts, Mimi Mahon, Karin W. Lager, Karen Harper, Jeri Kinneen, C. Karen Covey Moore, Michelle Linn-Gust, Valerie Tollini, Kathleen Willson, Lynn Klimo, Becky M. Bee, Fredda Wasserman, and Sarah Bergman. I especially thank my friends and family for their loving support.

Introduction

If you are reading this book, you have probably had someone close to you die by suicide or are helping the bereaved after a suicide. Published in 2000, the first edition of *But I Didn't Say Goodbye* is noted for providing its readers with insight on how best to help children after a suicide. The second edition is an empowering guidebook for bereaved children and families.

Suicide is a fatal self-inflicted destructive act. There is no one reason why someone dies by suicide. Suicide is the eleventh ranking cause of death for all ages. One of every 65 Americans has experienced a suicide of someone close to them. Annually, approximately 33,000 individuals die by suicide in the United States which is the equivalent of 89 suicides per day or one suicide every 16.1 minutes. Males die by suicide at nearly four times the rate of females. However, during their lifetime, women attempt suicide about two to three times as often as men. For females, the highest rate of suicide is among those in their forties and fifties. Men often use more violent means such as guns or hanging, and women more often use drugs or carbon monoxide poisoning.

Suicide is the eighth leading cause of death for males and the sixteenth leading cause for females. The highest rate of suicide is among males ages 75 years and older. The highest ranking suicide rate is in the western part of the U.S. followed by the South, Midwest, and Northeast. The highest ranking state for suicide is Montana, followed by Nevada and Alaska.

This book is designed for individuals who want to help children and families after a suicide. Children shouldn't read this book by themselves. I recommend that you read it first. The purpose of this book is to provide you with an overview of grief after a suicide and suggest interventions to assist you in caring for bereaved children and families.

What's in This Book

But I Didn't Say Goodbye is a book seen through the eyes of Alex, an eleven-year-old boy, whose father has died by suicide.

This story is a glimpse into a child's traumatic and life changing personal experience.

But I Didn't Say Goodbye introduces you to a bereaved family immediately after a suicide and ends five years later. The dialogue in each chapter will show you how you can help develop honest, open communication between children and the people in their lives. Alex's questions are the same as many other children following a suicide.

Chapter 1, The Worst Day, focuses on the difficulty and emotional strain involved in telling children that someone they loved has died by suicide. Chapter 2, The Next Day, identifies the concerns children may think about and share as they search for answers as to why someone died by suicide. Chapter 3, Talking About the Funeral, illustrates the process of explaining funeral ceremonies and burial procedures to children. Chapter 4, Telling a Friend What Happened, explores the importance of sharing one's story for the first time. You will compare the bereavement experience of a five-year-old child, an eleven-year-old adolescent and fourteen-year-old teenager. Chapter 5, A Mourning Ritual, focuses on healing rituals adults can share with bereaved children. Chapter 6, Grandma's Special Gift, shows the significance of giving bereaved children special objects that once belonged to the deceased. You will identify how objects, individuals, and locations are capable of making children feel safe. Chapter 7, When Grief Hurts, takes a look at the grief response in children after a suicide. You will list ways to explain the grief process to children to help them cope with their painful feelings. Chapter 8, Catching Up with Coach, focuses on caring adults recognizing fears in grieving children and explaining ways to cope with those fears. Chapter 9, One Month Later, describes issues related to blame. Chapter 10, Six Months Later, identifies the benefit of bereavement counseling. Chapter 11, One Year Anniversary, reviews the lessons that have helped shape a child's experience a year after the suicide. Chapter 12, Five Years Later, illustrates ways to cope with triggers and continue the bond with the deceased five years after the suicide.

Use this book in a way that works for you and the bereaved children and families you are helping. Children need adults they can rely on for honest answers based on age, emotional, and developmental level. Children may be reluctant to talk about the suicide. Shame and stigma may cloud the truth if the family has not been honest about what happened. Hoping to change the language in efforts to avoid the stigma of suicide, the phrase 'died by suicide' of 'died of suicide' is used throughout this book, rather than 'committed suicide.' 'Committed suicide' has been commonly used to describe when individuals take their own life. 'Died by suicide,' 'died of suicide,' 'died from suicide' or 'completed suicide' don't carry the stigma of criminality. This terminology is consistent with how people describe other types of death such as 'died of cancer' or 'died by accident', and thus died by suicide.

At the end of each chapter, you have a space for written expression, *Let's Identify Your Thoughts and Feelings*. These activities can be used in school counseling sessions, support groups, therapy sessions, or at home.

Finally, I offer a "Resources" section, which includes a statement of suicide loss rights, a list of books for bereaved children, teens, parents and professionals, bereavement resources and support after a suicide, information on how to locate adult bereavement support groups after a suicide, grief programs for children, teens, and families, sources to help you obtain financial information after a sudden death, and the national suicide prevention lifeline number.

On a Personal Note

Three weeks before I gave birth to triplets, my father died by suicide. I decided to share my story with you at the beginning of this book to illustrate how a person can take a tragedy and find meaning in it and through it, help others. I went into early labor and was in the hospital when I was told my dad was dead. I was in shock. I couldn't believe it. I was very close to my dad. He was always there for me, always accepting of me, always supportive and loving. He was part of my life; a part that I had taken for granted and believed would always be there.

I could not attend my dad's funeral. Doctor's Orders . . . Complete Bed Rest! How could I not attend his funeral or be a part of the rituals after his death? I had no choice. I needed to remain in bed and consider the health of my unborn triplets.

Three weeks later, my three sons were born. When visitors arrived at my hospital room, they congratulated me on the birth of the triplets and in the same breath told me how sorry they were about my dad's suicide. I didn't know how to feel. Was I supposed to be happy about being a new mom of triplets or sad because my dad killed himself? I was torn between the joy of having three healthy babies and the grief of knowing their grandfather would never hold them close or know them and they would never know him. Though it seemed so trivial, one of my biggest problems was the placement of cards I received from family and friends. Should I mix the sympathy cards with those that congratulated me on the birth of my triplets? Do I keep the cards separated on the hospital window shelf?

I remember looking at the open door of the hospital room anticipating my dad's visit. How could he not visit? How could he not see his three grandsons? Despite being kept busy taking care of my triplets, there always came the moment when my dad's death would surface. My friends and family were supportive. They told me my dad loved me, was proud of me, and was no longer in physical pain. Though they attempted to comfort me, the truth kept screaming at me, "But I didn't say goodbye."

While searching for meaning in my dad's death and meaning in my own life, I created and facilitated a support group for adults bereaved by suicide, became active in suicide prevention programs, and served as the Administrator for the NJ Chapter of the American Foundation for Suicide Prevention. I believe that everyone grieves in their own way. Bereavement intervention should be based on what works best for each person. Whether it's reading books about coping with grief and bereavement, attending support groups, or going to bereavement counseling, there is no one-size-fits-all approach to helping the bereaved. I have one aspiration . . . that you will walk away from *But I Didn't Say Goodbye* inspired and motivated to do something incredibly powerful . . . to care about children and families touched by suicide and have the tools to help them cope with their loss.

Foreword

Barbara Rubel's courageous work, *"But I Didn't Say Goodbye: Helping Children and Families After a Suicide"* is a beautifully written and pioneering resource for professionals, parents and children struggling with the difficult experience of helping children who have survived the suicide of a loved one.

This work is extremely accessible, simple, and developmentally appropriate for any child to read and be helped through its story line. The story spans the tragic suicide of the main character's father and takes the reader, step by step through the thoughts, feelings, and experiences a sudden death through suicide can bring.

The story applies the grief process through the family—we glimpse the raw emotions, and devastation the family experiences after such a shock and each chapter combines important exercises, questions, and applied activities to work through if the book is to be used professionally, by community groups, or parents.

There is no person better to address this difficult topic as Rubel has experienced the unimaginable, the loss of her dear father to suicide during her pregnancy. Rubel touches on the grieving process through children's fiction in a sensitive and heart-rendering manner.

Any person searching about how to help children through a suicide loss will be well served through this book as it applies and illustrates the differences in cognitive processes and the child's comprehension of the finality of death through the eyes of the two children, Alex and Debbie who are both at different developmental stages. It also illustrates the generational grief experiences of the family from grandparents, to spouse, to siblings and children.

Rubel has tackled this experience with sensitivity and grace. The anguish and sorrow of not being able to say goodbye after a death by suicide is addressed with care and compassion. This book will be of great benefit to families and communities alike.

—Julia Sorensen, MA, RPC, CCBT
Author and Therapist, *Overcoming Loss Stories and Activities for Children Experiencing Grief and Loss*

1

The Worst Day

Hi, my name is Alex. Let me tell you what happened five years ago, when I was in the fifth grade. It's not easy to talk about. Okay, so here goes. Every morning, my dad read the newspaper and drank coffee at the kitchen table. That morning, my dad was sitting at the table without his favorite coffee mug and the newspaper was nowhere in sight. My five-year-old sister, Debbie, was wearing her favorite pink dress. She was eating cereal as she watched TV. Anyway, I grabbed my book bag and lunch and walked right by Dad who was watching TV. He seemed in a very good mood. Dad hardly ever watched cartoons with Debbie. It was weird not seeing him drink his coffee or read his paper. I was late, so I ran out the door and down the street to my bus stop.

Right before lunch time, I was called out of my class. My teacher told me Uncle Sammy was in the office. She asked me to go to my locker and get my books and book bag. I was going home with my uncle. I always take the bus home. Why would

Uncle Sammy be taking me home early from school? He never picked me up before. I got my stuff and walked to the office. Uncle Sammy was sitting by the window. He was looking at his hands. When I walked in, the secretary told him I was there. He didn't seem like himself. When he saw me, he got up quickly and told me we had to get home.

"Uncle Sammy, why are you picking me up from school? What's going on?"

"We have to go. We have to get out of here," he yelled.

Uncle Sammy sounded angry. I never saw him like that. "Uncle Sammy, I don't get it. Why are you taking me home? Is something wrong? Where are Mom and Dad?"

As we walked toward the front entrance of the school, my uncle didn't answer any of my questions. The cold air made us rush toward his truck that much faster. The wind was so strong it almost knocked the both of us down. Uncle Sammy jingled his keys and kept looking down at the ground. He was usually upbeat and fun. Something wasn't right.

"Your mom asked me to come get you. Something did happen. Something big, something really . . . really . . . I'll explain it all to you at home." My uncle was shivering as he started the truck. He turned up the heat to make us both feel warmer.

"Uncle Sammy? You look funny. What's wrong?"

"Alex, stop! Just stop! Let me concentrate on getting us home. Just put your seat belt on please."

"No! I want to know what happened; you have to tell me what happened!" Frustrated, I reached for my seat belt as Uncle Sammy backed out of the parking lot. We didn't even make it off the school grounds when he turned toward me. Bursting out in tears, he drove to the side of the playground parking lot and shut off the engine.

"Oh my God, Alex, He's gone! He's . . ." Uncle Sammy's face got red and the tears came pouring out of his eyes. His words got caught in his throat. He started punching the steering wheel as he whispered, "Alex, your dad died this morning." It was strange seeing him punch the wheel and whisper at the same time. He took a very deep breath. "He's gone, Champ. He killed himself." Uncle Sammy was crying really hard as I sat there staring at him. He turned on the engine and buried his face in his hands.

I never saw my uncle like this. I was scared. I couldn't speak. As soon as I heard the words that Dad killed himself, my heart flipped over in my chest. How could my dad be dead? I really wanted to ask Uncle Sammy more questions, but I couldn't. Finally, I realized I could no longer hold it all in. My father killed himself. Uncle Sammy came all the way to school to pick me up because my dad was dead. I began to cry. Uncle Sammy wanted to calm me down. I know he did. All we could do was cry together. After hugging me, he kissed my forehead and drove home. I stared out the window. I felt like I wasn't even in the truck, like I was outside myself. This could not be happening to me.

Uncle Sammy parked in my driveway. I got out of the truck and slammed the door. It felt as though I was moving in slow motion. Was my dad really dead? Was this some awful dream? Would I wake up any minute? Although my uncle told me that Dad died by suicide, parts of me were still uncertain. With each step I took toward the house, the faster my heart began to race. By the time I reached the front door I was certain my heart would just burst out of my chest. Mom was on the phone, sitting at the kitchen table. Debbie was drawing a picture and the table was covered in crayons. Mom's face was really puffy. Her eyes were red. She was talking to someone about Dad. I heard her whisper, "Yes, a traditional service; closed casket . . . Thank you." I guess she was arranging my dad's funeral. When she saw me looking at her, she quickly hung up the phone.

"Mom, what happened to Dad?" She got up from the table and hugged me tighter than she ever had before.

"Let's sit down on the couch, Alex. I have to talk to you." As we both sat down, I felt like I was moving in slow motion. "I have some very bad news. Daddy died by suicide. He killed himself."

"Why would Dad kill himself?"

"I keep asking myself the same question," Mom replied as she softly rubbed my hand and looked down at the floor. "One thing is for certain, Daddy had some serious problems. He was suffering from depression. I just never thought he would kill himself."

As much as I didn't want to ask her, I couldn't hold back. "How did he do it?"

"Daddy shot himself with his gun."

"No, Mom, no! You're lying! Why would you say such a horrible lie like that?"

"I can't believe it either, Alex."

"Were you here with him when he did it, Mom? Did you see him?"

"No, Alex. He was by himself."

"Where were you, Mom?"

"I was in the laundry room folding clothes when I heard a loud noise. I didn't know what it was. It sounded like it came from the basement."

"What did you do?"

"I called out for Dad. When he didn't answer, I rushed down to the basement and found him dead on the floor."

"Where was the gun?"

"The gun was near his side. I looked at his face and saw he had shot himself in his head."

"Daddy shot himself in his head?"

Taking several deep breaths, Mom continued, "Daddy wasn't breathing. I checked his heart and it wasn't beating. His heart stopped. I knew he was dead."

"I don't believe it, Mom."

"I couldn't believe it, either."

"Mom, did you call 911?"

"I called 911 right away. I did CPR, but Dad was dead. The ambulance was here within minutes. There was nothing the Emergency Medical Team could do to save him."

"Where is he now? Where is Daddy?"

"His body is at the funeral home." As we sat on the couch, she whispered, "Everything is going to be okay." I said nothing. Mom held on like she would never let me go. I felt a little stiff as she hugged me even though I very much wanted to hold on tight. "I love you so much," she said as she began to cry. It felt as though we were on the couch like that for hours as she tried her best to explain what happened to Dad.

I wondered if any of this was my fault. "Mom, did Daddy kill himself because of something I did?"

✱"Nothing you said or did could have ever caused your dad to do such a thing. Don't you ever forget that. We will try to figure it all out. This did not happen because of anything you did or did not do!"

No matter how much Mom told me it wasn't my fault, I didn't believe her. The bottom line was, I still needed answers. I needed to know why my dad killed himself. Was he sick of me always being late for the bus? Was he angry at me for always asking him to help me with my homework? I knew something was different this morning. But it didn't stop me from leaving. I should have stayed home. What was so wrong with Dad's life that he would do this to himself . . . and to me?

Alex shared his story with you. When you are ready, you can share your story with an adult. Here are some questions and activities to explore . . .

Let's Identify
Your Thoughts and Feelings

What kinds of thoughts are going through your mind right now?

What did Chapter 1 make you think about?

If you think Uncle Sammy could have explained to Alex what happened any differently, what should he have said?

What do you think of Alex's mom's explanation about what happened?

Have you had an experience similar to Alex? If so, what was that experience?

How old were you when this person died?

What was your relationship with the person who died?

Who was it that told you this person had died?

What did you feel toward the person who told you about the death?

You just finished Chapter 1. Take a moment to relax and think. Focus on how your body feels. Is any part tense or uncomfortable? Notice the emotions you are experiencing. What are they? Are you feeling any strong emotions now? Name them. Find an adult to talk to, or write or draw something about your feelings. Do you want to read the next chapter now or do you want to take a break? If you take a break, find something fun or relaxing to do.

2

The Next Day

Before my dad's death, I had a certain routine every morning. My usual day started out with me thinking about breakfast. This day was different. When I woke up, my first thoughts were all about my dad. He was dead. I was thinking about how Dad would not be at the kitchen table. He would not be lighting the fireplace. Dad always lit the fireplace. Did my mom even know how to light it? Although it was a school day, Mom asked Debbie and me if we wanted to stay home. We told her that we didn't want to go to school. A part of me was happy that I didn't have to go out in the freezing weather. I was not going to school. Another part of me felt guilty. I was staying home because yesterday my dad died.

I felt anxious while I ate my breakfast with Debbie, Mom and Uncle Sammy. My uncle took the day off from work to be with us. I had a headache. Dad should have been sitting in his chair. He should have been reading the newspaper and drinking coffee from his favorite mug. It was his routine. My daily routine of getting up and having cereal will probably never change. I guess the only thing that has changed is that he will no longer eat his cereal beside me or talk to me ever again.

My sister, Debbie, handed me a *Junie B. Jones* book. She got it for her birthday. "Read to me, Alex." The book had a picture of a girl wearing a pink bunny costume.

"Hey, Deb, didn't you wear a costume like this for Halloween?"

"Yeah," she said as she giggled, making me smile.

"I'll read it to you later today. I promise. First, let me finish my cereal."

"Okay Alex . . . you promise?"

"I promise, Debbie." As I ate my cereal, I told my uncle and my mom about last night. It was a strange night. I felt sad and mixed up inside as I tried to go to sleep. I began to wonder if I was always going to feel this way. I wished I could go to sleep and wake up and find out it never happened. I barely slept all night. Every time I woke up, I was hoping it was just a bad dream. Then I would remember the nightmare was real.

During the night, something made me get up. I thought I saw Dad standing by my bed. I really felt like he was in my bedroom. I know he couldn't actually be in the room. But I felt like he was there. As soon as I got up, his image was gone. I went back to sleep. The last thing I thought about as I fell asleep was seeing Dad at the kitchen table the morning he died. He wasn't reading the paper. He wasn't drinking coffee. Maybe I should have known something wasn't right.

As I was eating my cereal, I felt scared. I don't know what I was afraid of. I was confused and angry and sad all at once. It felt like a typical morning in my house while at the same time, nothing felt the same. While eating breakfast, Uncle Sammy looked through our photo albums. He had tears in his eyes but a smile on his face. I thought about the times Dad and I would put new photos in the album. He would sit in his favorite chair. I would hand him the photos. One by one, Dad would place each photo in the album. Afterwards we would play ball out back, while Mom and Debbie looked over our work. When I was little, Dad gave me the nickname "Champ." I will never forget how special that name made me feel.

"Uncle Sammy, I keep thinking Dad will come home soon. I can't stop thinking about him."

"I'm thinking about him too, Champ."

"Well, that makes three of us," Mom added.

"One, two, three, four," Debbie said.

"You're right, Deb. All four of us are thinking about Daddy," Mom said.

After I finished my breakfast, I went over to the couch and sat down to watch TV. Mom and Uncle Sammy were washing dishes. I wasn't trying to listen to their conversation, but from what I could hear they were talking about real estate and bills.

He looked over at me and asked, "Alex, what are you thinking about over there? Somebody's awfully quiet."

"Dad told me he was going to watch me in my school play next week. My fifth grade class is putting on a show for the entire grade. All the parents are invited."

"What's it about?"

"The play is about the Constitution. I will be talking about the judicial part of the government."

"Aw, man," Uncle Sammy exclaimed, "Your dad always talked about how good you were in your school plays and how you never missed a line. I know your dad would have loved to see you in the play."

I felt angry. If my dad loved to see me in the plays he wouldn't have killed himself. If he really loved me . . . , I thought. The more we talked about it, the angrier I started to feel.

"I think your dad will be watching you from heaven. I believe that whenever you are in a play, he will be there with you. I'm really sorry your dad died by suicide. That wasn't supposed to happen. He's supposed to be here and go to your school play."

"It did happen, Uncle Sammy. I don't get it. One day he was here and the next day he's gone. He helped me when I practiced my lines about the judicial part of the constitution. We worked on that part together. Why would he kill himself before the show? Why didn't he wait to see me in my school show?"

"It was a huge mistake! Your dad was suffering from depression. He felt hopeless. He wasn't thinking clearly. He was just hurting so much."

"This hurts so much, Uncle Sammy."

"When someone you love dies, it hurts very much. It sounds like you're angry with Dad, too. Your dad was not thinking clearly."

"It just doesn't make sense. How could this happened? My dad should have come to me for help."

"It doesn't make sense. He didn't come to me either! Why did he do it? I just don't know, Alex, I just don't know." Mom walked into the room and sat down. I began wondering maybe if I would have stayed home from school yesterday, or if I had been better or nicer to Dad, he wouldn't have killed himself. I was starting to worry about things I never thought of before. "Hey Champ, I have an idea. How about we go out for some hot cocoa?" Mom, totally taken off guard asked, "Who? You and Alex?"

"No, all four of us should go out for cocoa. No matter how long we all sit around with our heads down, feeling like this, nothing is going to change. Maybe you and the kids need some Montana air. The sun's come out. Let's get out of the house."

"It's freezing!" she said.

"Please, Mom. Let's take a ride and get cocoa." Mom agreed and went upstairs with Debbie to get dressed. I blurted out, "Uncle Sammy, was it my fault?"

"What makes you think it could be your fault?"

"Maybe I should have been a better kid."

"A better kid?"

"Yeah, maybe I shouldn't have been asking Dad so many questions about the branches of government this week. I should have known. I should have stayed home from school and done something."

"Your dad's suicide was not your fault. Your dad's depression wasn't your fault either. Listen, your dad obviously had bigger problems than your mom and I were even aware of," Uncle Sammy assured me.

"Mom should have done something to save him."

"She had no idea he was going to die of suicide. She was doing laundry," Uncle Sammy said.

"If she wasn't doing laundry she would have seen him with his gun. She could have saved him."

"Your dad went into the basement so she would not see him. It was not your mom's fault," he assured me.

"I'm mad at her. I'm mad at Dad. He should be here. He should be going to my school play next week. Every dad will be there but him!"

"I'm glad you're talking to me about your feelings. I think you should also talk with Mom. Do you think I can go to your school and watch you in your play next week?"

"Yeah, sure." Even though it would be fine for my uncle to watch me in the show, I wanted my dad to watch me. I felt angry that my uncle would be there and not my dad. "I'll let you know the day and time, Uncle Sammy. But, I just don't know if I'll still be in the same school."

"Same school? What makes you think you won't be in the same school?" Uncle Sammy looked totally puzzled.

"I don't know. Maybe we'll have to move because Mom can't afford to pay the bills."

"Wow, bills! Champ, what on earth would put that idea in your head?" Just then my uncle looked down at the floor and thought for a second. It was no secret in our family that at times I was known for listening to the grown-up conversations.

"That's not a problem, Alex. Mom can afford to live in this house with you and your sister. It's important for you to feel safe. I love you, your mother and Deb so much. I promise you that I'm here to look out for all of you. Everything will be okay."

As I listened to Uncle Sammy I thought to myself that everything was not okay. My dad's dead! Before I knew it, Mom and Debbie were coming down the stairs. I went to reach for my coat and sneakers; we were going out for cocoa.

We went to the same diner that Dad would take us to. It felt strange to sit in the booth without him. On the way back from the diner, we stopped at a store and picked up more cocoa to have in the house. Mom, Uncle Sammy and Debbie went inside and I decided to stay outside and fly my helicopter. It had a cockpit cabin and a strobe light. My dad taught me how to use the transmitter and how to fix the blades. After a while, my hands felt like they were frozen to the radio control. So, I went inside for some more hot cocoa.

I walked into the kitchen and Mom said, "Please get your helicopter off the table. We don't have any room in here for food let alone helicopters." Mom was right. The kitchen was filled with flowers. It also had big baskets of fruit. We even had three tuna casseroles in the refrigerator.

About an hour later, Dad's doctor called Mom. After they spoke, she stared out the kitchen window and said, "Maybe the doctor should have changed his medication. I don't know. The doctor did the right thing in calling me to offer his condolences."

"What's that, Mom?"

"Condolences. It sure is a big word. Condolence is an expression of sympathy, Alex. It's when friends and neighbors

show they care about us by sending food, flowers, and cards."
Just then, the door bell rang. As Mom opened the door, I
saw Uncle Gary and Aunt Jennifer. Uncle Gary was Dad's
youngest brother. They stood in the hall taking turns hugging
Mom and Uncle Sammy. He and my aunt lived in Las Vegas.
Mom and Dad had fun whenever they visited them. My dad
promised me that he would take me to Las Vegas when I turned
21. He would not be keeping his promise. As I hugged my aunt
and uncle, I realized Uncle Gary looked so much like my dad.
It made me feel really sad. Debbie ran into the hall and gave
everyone hugs. She wanted to show Aunt Jennifer and Uncle
Gary photos from Disney World. Only a few months had
passed since our aunt and uncle met us in Florida. We had
a great time on vacation. But now, it seems like such a long
time ago.

"Oh yeah, show us the photos," Uncle Gary said as he and
my aunt sat down on the couch in the living room.

As Debbie went to get the album, Uncle Gary asked
Mom, "How are you? How are the kids holding up?" Uncle
Gary grabbed a handful of nuts and a pear from one of the
fruit baskets.

"What can I say? This is definitely the worst of times.
Gary, he's gone. My husband, my friend, my world—he's gone
forever. How could he do this to me? I don't understand
why. Why would he kill himself?"

"He must have felt helpless. Did you speak with his
doctor?" my aunt asked.

"Yes, I did. The doctor seemed sincere. I think he really
felt terrible about what happened. But, I mean, why didn't
the medicine work? Why didn't his doctor see the warning
signs? Why didn't he do something? Sure, he was sorry.
He talked about depression and brain chemicals. I felt
comforted by what he said, but I'm angry with him,"
Mom said.

"What are you angry about? Doctors can only do so much. We can only do so much. Truthfully, we can sit here and try to figure it all out, but in the end, we all did what we could with what we had," Aunt Jennifer sighed.

"And what was that?" Mom asked in between sniffles.

"Our love. We gave him our love," My aunt whispered.

"Yeah, we sure did. I knew my brother suffered from depression since we were teenagers and believe me, I loved him through some very hard times," Uncle Gary added.

Debbie came back into the room with her album. We looked at the photos. Mom started to laugh as she saw the photo of Dad wearing Mickey Mouse ears.

Touching my arm, Uncle Gary said, "Your dad looked happy. You would never know how depressed he really was. His depression sometimes made him hurt so much inside. He just wasn't thinking clearly."

Alex shared his story with you. When you are ready, you can share your story with an adult. Here are some questions and activities to explore . . .

Let's Identify Your Thoughts and Feelings

What kinds of thoughts are going through your mind right now?

What did Chapter 2 make you think about?

If you had a certain routine that changed after the person died, explain how it changed for the better or for the worse.

If you have any thoughts like Alex, can you describe them?

How does it feel to have to deal with these thoughts?

Who can you talk to about these thoughts?

Create a list of 3 situations that you are most worried about.

Is anyone in your family worried about the same things you are worried about? If so, describe what that person is worried about and how he or she is coping.

Draw a picture of what you are worrying about today.

If anyone expressed their sympathy to you, what did they say or do?

How did what they say or do make you feel?

Who was the person that discussed the reasons why someone dies by suicide?

How did the person explain why someone dies by suicide?

What was the hardest time for you after the death?

What made you feel better during this time?

List as many people as you can who would be there for you if you ever felt really sad or hopeless.

You just finished Chapter 2. Take a moment to relax and think. Focus on how your body feels. Is any part tense or uncomfortable? Notice the emotions you are experiencing. What are they? Are you feeling any strong emotions now? Name them. Find an adult to talk to, or write or draw something about your feelings. Do you want to read the next chapter now or do you want to take a break? If you take a break, find something fun or relaxing to do.

3

Talking About the Funeral

Uncle Sammy was sitting in Dad's chair talking to my mom, my aunt and my uncle. I wondered if I would always think of that chair as *Dad's chair*. Mom was asking Uncle Sammy to deliver the eulogy at Dad's funeral. It was going to be a graveside service. Mom wanted him to say a few words about Dad at the graveside. My uncle was having a very hard time. He wanted to talk about his brother, but he kept saying he didn't think he'd be able to get the words out. Uncle Sammy knew for sure that he would break down in front of everyone.

"Uncle Sammy, I think Dad would have wanted you to speak at his service."

"I don't know what to say, Champ."

"Just tell everyone what it was that made you two close," Mom added, "Share a funny story. Think back on what you admired most about him."

"Admire? I'm so angry at what he did. Admiring my brother is the last thing on my mind."

"I know you're angry. We're all shattered by this. Believe me. I mean . . . I lost the light of my life. He was your brother. For crying out loud, he was my husband!" I watched her as she took a deep breath and cooled down. Pouring a glass of tea, she softened her tone. "Please, Sammy, I honestly think that in the long run, you will look back and be glad you did the eulogy."

"I don't think I'll ever be glad again," Uncle Sammy sighed.

"Uncle Sammy, I'll help you. I have lots of memories of you and Dad teaching me about baseball, and going fishing, or to the movies."

"That would be tons of memories, Alex. I'll work on it. I'll come up with something. I think I'm going to talk about what I'll miss the most about him. I can do it."

"Sam, the eulogy will only take about ten minutes. You'll be okay," Mom said.

"Uncle Sammy, write out what you want to say first. That's what I do before I work on a speech that I have to give to my class."

"That's good thinking, Alex," Uncle Sammy replied.

"I'm also thinking about the funeral and what's going to happen. Mom explained it all to me already, but part of me still feels nervous."

"What did your mom tell you?" Uncle Sammy asked.

"We'll be going to the funeral home. That's where Daddy's body is. His body will be washed and placed in a wooden box."

"Right, Alex. It's called a casket."

"Some caskets are made out of metal. Mom chose a wooden one. The casket will be kept closed. Mom said it will be placed in a special car called a hearse. The hearse will be driven to the cemetery. All the cars going to the cemetery will follow behind the hearse. All car headlights stay on."

"It's called a funeral procession. It's a time to honor your dad, Alex," Mom added.

Uncle Sammy patted me on my back and said, "I'm proud of you, Alex. You're a good listener."

"I gave you a lot of information about Dad's funeral," Mom whispered.

"Yeah, you did, Mom."

"I hope it makes it easier for you to understand what's going to happen," she said.

"What else did Mom tell you about the funeral?" Uncle Sammy asked.

"She said it's going to be sad. Dad's friends are going to be there, too. We're all going to stand around the grave."

"What did Mom tell you about the actual grave?"

"It's a large hole dug out of the dirt. Daddy's casket will be placed over the hole."

"Did Mom tell you what happens next?"

"She said that the casket is put into the grave. We'll take a shovel and toss dirt onto the top of the casket. That's it."

"Yeah, that's it. The cemetery workers will completely cover the casket with dirt after we leave," Uncle Sammy added.

As she finished her tea, Mom asked, "Alex, would you like to tell Uncle Sammy about the service and what people will be doing at your dad's funeral?"

"Some people will be crying, some will be whispering, some will not say a word. Everyone will say goodbye to my dad in their own way."

"Then we'll go back to the house and it's over," Uncle Sammy sighed.

Mom continued to explain things, "After the funeral, everyone will gather at our home, eat, and share their loss—Dad's death. When we go back to the cemetery in a few months, there will be a headstone over the grave. We talked about this already. I just want to make sure you know what to expect."

"I know, Mom. I've seen headstones in movies."

"It's probably just like in the movies. The headstone will have Daddy's name, birthday, and date of death on it. I'm thinking of having the words, *Loving Husband, Father, Son, Brother and Friend* engraved on the stone."

"I want to do something at the funeral, Mom. Uncle Sammy is doing something. I just don't know what I can do."

"You can share a favorite memory. You can write Dad a letter. I can place it in the casket."

"Can I put two rocks in the casket, metamorphic and igneous rocks?"

"Meta . . . what?" Mom asked, seeming totally confused.

"Rocks, Mom, I'm talking about rocks. Daddy would understand," I whispered.

"Yeah, Champ, I know he would," Uncle Sammy added.

"I also have a picture of me and Dad fishing. I want him to have it."

"Alex, I'll make sure the rocks and the picture are placed in his casket."

"I'm going to ask Deb to draw a picture and have that placed in the casket, too." Mom said.

"Is Debbie going?" Uncle Sammy asked.

"Sam, I believe that no child is too young to attend a funeral, especially if the person who died is their dad. I'll explain everything to her so she isn't afraid or confused."

Debbie came into the room. She wanted to go outside and play in the snow. I told Mom that I would give her the rocks and picture when we came back from playing outside. I got my jacket, hat, and gloves and we both ran for the door.

Alex shared his story with you. When you are ready, you can share your story with an adult. Here are some questions and activities to explore . . .

Let's Identify
Your Thoughts and Feelings

What kinds of thoughts are going through your mind right now?

What did Chapter 3 make you think about?

If someone recited a eulogy for the person who died, what did he or she say?

How did their special words make you feel?

If you could recite a eulogy for the person who died, what would you say?

What did the casket look like?

Was the casket open or closed at the funeral home?

If anything special was placed in the casket, describe it.

What was the hardest part of the funeral for you?

If you did not attend the funeral, how did you feel about not going?

If you had a member of the clergy at the funeral, what did he or she say that brought you comfort?

If the person was cremated, describe the type of urn used.

You just finished Chapter 3. Take a moment to relax and think. Focus on how your body feels. Is any part tense or uncomfortable? Notice the emotions you are experiencing. What are they? Are you feeling any strong emotions now? Name them. Find an adult to talk to, or write or draw something about your feelings. Do you want to read the next chapter now or do you want to take a break? If you take a break, find something fun or relaxing to do.

4

Telling a Friend What Happened

Debbie and I played outside in the snow. Debbie was making snow angels, singing her happy birthday song over and over again. I made a few snowballs and threw them at Debbie's snowman. The carrot on the snowman's face was drooping down his chin. Debbie jumped up from the snow and threw a snowball. It ended up knocking the carrot right off his face.

"Great shot, Deb!" I yelled. When I managed to catch my breath from laughing, I looked up and noticed my neighbor, Brian, walking toward us. Brian was fourteen years old. Although he was a few years older than me, we would hang out together. He had two older brothers, Alan and Michael. They were both in college and lived in a dorm in New Jersey. I wasn't ready to tell Brian about my dad. I wanted to stop playing and run into my house. I wanted to hide. My heart was beating fast. I was scared to death as Brian stared at me. Did he know about my dad?

Brian said, "I was home from school yesterday because I had a stomachache. I saw a police car outside of your house. What happened?"

I didn't want to answer his question. I didn't want to talk about the police. I didn't want to talk about Dad's suicide. But, Brian was my friend. I figured it would be okay to tell him what happened. "My dad died while I was at school," I replied, as my hands started shaking in my coat pockets.

"What happened? Was he in an accident?"

"No. There was no accident," I whispered. It was hard to say—but, I said it, "Nothing like that. My dad died by suicide. He killed himself."

"He killed himself? Aw, man, I'm sorry, Alex. Why did he do it?"

"He was depressed. My mom said he was in a lot of pain. My dad wasn't thinking right. My mom said his brain had a disease. My uncles said he was hopeless and helpless." As I looked up, I saw Debbie sucking her thumb. Debbie stopped sucking her thumb when she was three years old. Debbie told me she wanted to go inside the house.

Sounding like a baby, she said, "I want my mommy," as she ran into the house.

"See ya later, Deb," Brian said.

Talking to Brian about what happened wasn't as bad as I thought. My heart was still beating fast, but I felt relieved.

Brian continued, "I just finished reading a book where one of the characters killed himself after hearing strange voices in his head. My cousin, Eileen, died by suicide. I think she may have heard voices, too."

Right then, something clicked in my head. Suicide can happen to anyone. It happens to other kids too. "Wait, your cousin died, too?"

"Yeah, she died. Eileen killed herself last year. She hanged herself."

"How old was she?"

"She was fifteen."

"My mom told me my dad was clinically depressed. What was your cousin's problem?"

"I don't know much. After she died, her dad, my Uncle Matthew, said she was impulsive. Eileen was doing drugs. I overheard her dad tell my parents she would cut herself. She had scars on her arms. No one ever talks about her anymore. I remember the last time I saw her at a barbeque. She looked scary. I couldn't even understand her when she talked to me. Nothing she said made sense. She was talking back to my Uncle Matthew and Aunt Esther. She gave me a big hug and whispered, 'It's just not worth it, Brian. I'm thinking about going away.' I loved my cousin. I had no idea she was talking about killing herself. I didn't get it. I still want to talk about her, but every time I bring up her name, my family changes the subject."

"Is it because your family is mad at her?"

"I don't know. No one talks about her," Brian explained.

"Maybe they're mad at her."

"I think they're probably mad she killed herself. But since they avoid talking about her, I don't know. Sometimes, I think they're mad at me. Maybe they think I could have saved her. Maybe they think I should have talked to her about her problems. Maybe they think I didn't do everything I could to save her. Maybe everyone is mad at me for not helping her."

"Brian, if your family talked about her, you wouldn't be worrying so much."

"That's just it, Alex," Brian continued. "I worry about everything."

"You're the first friend I told about what happened to my dad. I don't want to keep it a secret. Is your family keeping Eileen's suicide a secret?"

"No . . . I don't think so. I don't know. It's confusing. No one tells me anything!"

"I'm confused too, Brian."

"I want to talk about her. My parents, my aunts, and my uncles don't want to."

"Tomorrow, I'll be going to my dad's funeral. Did you go to Eileen's funeral?"

"No, I didn't go. My mother said that I couldn't go to the funeral because everyone would be crying and upset. Both of my parents didn't want me to go through that."

"Did you want to go to the funeral?"

"Yeah, I did. Kids don't go to funerals in my family. It's not allowed. I talked to my cousins about it. It's totally unfair. How are we supposed to deal with death if our family doesn't include us? I don't get it, Alex, I just don't get it."

"My mom asked me and Debbie if we wanted to go to the funeral. We want to go. Mom explained everything to us. She told us that we will say prayers. A few of Dad's friends will talk about him. She said that we'll celebrate his life. Then his casket will be placed in the ground."

"The hearse will probably take your dad's body to the cemetery."

"My mom told me about the hearse. It's a large, black car that will take the casket to the cemetery. That's the place where my dad's casket will be put in the ground. I can't believe he will be inside a casket," I sighed, as I shook my head.

"Your dad's body will be in the casket. He's in heaven, Alex."

"Brian, you sound like my mom. Were you mad at God for letting your cousin die?"

"No, I wasn't mad at God. I was mad at Eileen for not telling me she was thinking about suicide. The day she told me that it wasn't worth it and she was thinking of going away, I thought she meant not doing drugs any more and going to camp or something. I'm not sure what I could have done to save her. But, I would have tried. I'm mad at her sometimes. I'm mad at my family for not letting me go to the funeral."

"Honestly, part of me can't believe I'm going to my dad's funeral. This is unreal, Brian. God, I can't believe this is happening."

"Are you mad at God, Alex?"

"I think God should have helped my dad stay alive."

"Do you want to come over to my house?" Brian asked.

"Yeah! You know what? That sounds like a great idea. I'll be right back. I'll tell my mom I'm going to your house to hang out."

When I walked in the kitchen, my mom was talking about the funeral with my family. "There you are, Champ!" Mom exclaimed, as she greeted me. "Sit down. I made buffalo wings." As Mom took out bleu cheese and ranch dressing, she said, "You must be hungry."

"Well, actually, Mom," I interrupted. "I'm still pretty full from breakfast."

"Oh, get real, Alex. Breakfast was hours ago. You've been playing in that cold snow all morning. Debbie told me you were out there talking to Brian."

"But Mom . . ."

"But Mom, what, Alex? I'd really like for you to sit down, warm up, and eat lunch."

"I want to go hang out with Brian."

"Have a quick bite first. Then go. But don't stay late. Tomorrow is Dad's funeral."

While I was calling Brian to tell him that I was going to eat and then come over, I saw Debbie sucking her thumb. Deb asked, "Is Daddy going to the funeral, too?"

"Daddy is dead, honey. We're all going to Daddy's funeral. His body will be in a casket. Remember, his body will be in a wooden box . . ." Mom re-explained.

"What is Daddy going to do all the time when he's dead?"

"Daddy's body doesn't work anymore. He won't be doing anything. That's why his body will be inside the box and placed in the ground," Mom explained.

As I finished my last wing, I said, "How many times do you have to tell Debbie the same thing?"

"Debbie is not as old as you, Alex. It's hard for her to understand what's happening."

"She's five. Why is she sucking her thumb, Mom? Deb hasn't done that in a long time."

"Debbie is sad that Daddy died. Sucking her thumb again makes her feel better. It's her way of coping with Daddy's death. It's okay."

"I don't care. I'm sick of talking about coping. I'm sick of talking about Dad's death. I'm sick of listening to you talk about it over and over again, Mom. I'm out of here," I said as I headed out the door.

Firmly, Mom responded, "Alex, wait a minute. I know you're upset. So am I. But you still need to be respectful."

"I'm sorry, Mom."

Sounding like a three-year-old, Debbie said, "Daddy died. Mommy told me that everybody dies."

"All living things die. Just like the dead deer we saw on the road the other day. He was alive. Then he got hit by a car. He died. We don't know when it's going to happen. Everyone dies sooner or later," Mom explained.

"Did Daddy get hit by a car?" Debbie asked.

"No, Daddy took his own life. He used a gun to make his body stop working."

"Make Daddy come alive again," Debbie demanded.

"Once you're dead, you can't come back to life."

"How long is Daddy going to be dead?"

Mom whispered, "Debbie, Daddy is going to be dead forever. I believe even though his body died, his spirit will go to heaven. We talked about this, Deb."

Debbie started to cry. As Mom put Debbie on her lap and hugged her real tight, Mom started to cry. As they held each other, I heard Debbie whisper, "Why did Daddy leave me?"

"Daddy was hurting inside. He wasn't thinking right. Daddy loved you very much," Mom reassured her.

I got up from the table to go over to Brian's house. "Mom, I'll be back soon. Okay?"

"Where are you going?"

"Mom, I already told you. I'm going to hang out with Brian."

"Oh yeah, right. Before you go, Alex, I want to ask you something. I'm going to go through Daddy's clothes and will pick out a suit for him to be buried in. Do you want to help me pick out his clothes?"

"No, I don't think so."

"You sure?" Mom asked.

I thought for a moment and said, "Mom, I think he liked his navy suit best."

Mom nodded her head in agreement. "That's a good choice. Your dad looked handsome in that suit. Thank you for helping me."

I was glad Brian asked me to come over. It was good to get out of the house for a little while. Brian had a cool poster on his ceiling over his bed that read, "*The difficult we do today. The impossible takes a little longer*"—the motto of the U.S. Army Corps of Engineers. I realized what I was going through was really hard. I couldn't imagine anything worse until I thought of tomorrow, Dad's funeral.

Brian took his hamster, Marty, from the cage and put him in a small plastic ball. Marty ran so fast, the ball was all over the floor. We watched Marty as he sat in the middle of the plastic ball. He used both of his tiny hands to clean his face.

"I have an idea. Let's feed him some nuts," Brian said.

Brian got Marty out of the plastic ball and held him in his hands. Marty didn't eat any of the nuts. Instead, he put each nut in his cheeks. Before we knew it, his two cheeks were filled with nuts. We laughed so hard that we fell down. Brian almost dropped Marty. He caught him just in time. Brian put Marty in the cage. We watched him remove each nut from his cheeks by touching both sides of his face. In those few minutes watching Marty, I didn't think of my dad, his suicide, or how sad I was. I didn't think about his funeral tomorrow. I didn't think about anything that made me upset. I wasn't sure if it was okay to laugh. I felt a little guilty. I thought about it. I figured my dad would want me to enjoy my life and do what kids do best, have a good time. After awhile, I went home and Uncle Sammy's truck was still in the driveway. It reminded me of when he picked me up from school the day my dad died.

Alex shared his story with you. When you are ready, you can share your story with an adult. Here are some questions and activities to explore . . .

Let's Identify Your Thoughts and Feelings

What kinds of thoughts are going through your mind right now?

What did Chapter 4 make you think about?

What are three things you miss the most about the person who died?

What was the most difficult thing you ever had to deal with in your life?

After the person in your family died, who was the first person you told what happened?

What were your thoughts, feelings and reactions before, during, and after sharing the bad news for the first time?

Do you think adults in your family should talk with children about death?

Do you think adults in your family should allow children to attend funerals?

If you were ever asked to keep a secret, how did it make you feel?

Do you know what the person was wearing in the casket? Do you know why that clothing was chosen?

Did the clothing have special meaning for you? for others? Please explain.

In what ways have you had fun since the person died?

Do you think the person who died would want you to have fun?

If you had fun or laughed about something after the person died, did you feel guilty? Please explain.

You just finished Chapter 4. Take a moment to relax and think. Focus on how your body feels. Is any part tense or uncomfortable? Notice the emotions you are experiencing. What are they? Are you feeling any strong emotions now? Name them. Find an adult to talk to, or write or draw something about your feelings. Do you want to read the next chapter now or do you want to take a break? If you take a break, find something fun or relaxing to do.

5

A Mourning Ritual

Mom was sitting at the dining room table with my aunt and uncles. She was wearing a black dress. I never saw her wear it before. I sat down and kept staring at Mom. "Alex, what's on your mind?" she asked.

"Why are you dressed like that?"

"I should have talked to you about this before. I'm sorry. I take so many things for granted. How would you know about our mourning custom if I don't tell you about it?"

"Mourning?"

"Yeah, mourning. It's not the same as when you get up in the morning. People in mourning act a certain way based on their culture or religion. They share their feelings with family, friends and their community."

"We share our feelings, Mom."

"Yes we do. People in mourning may eat special foods or wear certain clothes. I'm wearing black because it's my mourning ritual and I can't count the number of people who sent us food."

"Food? Are you kidding? In just one day we had so many people give us fruit baskets and tuna casseroles."

"Exactly. Neighbors and friends care about you. Bringing food to our home is a mourning custom. Sometimes people send flowers or money to a charity in memory of the person who died. Daddy's office sent a donation in his memory to an organization that helps prevent suicide."

"That's nice, Mom."

She nodded and responded, "One of Dad's co-workers stopped by on his way to work. He gave me a picture of Dad. It was taken at last year's company Christmas party. He was dressed up as an elf."

"You've got to be kidding. Mom, I have to see it."

"I've got to see that!" Uncle Sammy said.

"I'll show it to you both. I might take it out each December as a reminder of the funny things your dad would do. It could become a ritual."

"What's a ritual, Mom?"

"A ritual is a pattern or a routine. Every morning you brush your teeth. Every night, I read a book to Debbie. These are rituals. Sometimes a ritual is only done once. Other times a ritual is done more often."

"Yeah, I guess I have a few rituals, too."

"A ritual can help you feel safe and in control. We can create a ritual that can help us honor Daddy and remember him. If every December I look at the picture that was taken of him at his Christmas party, I make that act a ritual."

"Let's do a ritual for Dad."

"You and your sister can light a candle with me. We can say a prayer or recite a poem. This could be our family ritual."

"I'd like that, Mom."

"Obviously, for safety reasons, it's important to only light candles when adults are with you."

"I know. Can we do it today?"

"We sure can. We can do it whenever we need to. We can also take out the photo album and look at it together."

"Okay, Mom."

"Also, the intention behind all of these rituals is not only to remember, but to celebrate your dad's life," Uncle Gary said.

"Mom, do you remember my scrapbook with my awards, report cards and pictures of me with my teams?"

"Sure, Alex. It's a great scrapbook."

"I'm going to add things that belonged to Daddy to that scrapbook."

"That's a great idea. I had a scrapbook when I was a kid. I'll have to look for it. I would love to show it to you."

"Mom, do you have anything of Daddy's that I could have for my scrapbook?"

"I can give you his driver's license and some pictures of him."

"I might have a few things to give you, too," Uncle Sammy said.

"That's great. Thanks."

I grabbed my scrapbook from the shelf. I started writing words on top of the pages that reminded me of Dad. I wrote, *"Sports Dad Liked", "Dad's Hobbies", "Dad's Favorite Animals", "What Dad Liked to Do on the Weekend", "One Silly Thing I Know about Dad", "Dad's Favorite Food"*.

Alex shared his story with you. When you are ready, you can share your story with an adult. Here are some questions and activities to explore . . .

Let's Identify
Your Thoughts and Feelings

What kinds of thoughts are going through your mind right now?

What did Chapter 5 make you think about?

Create a scrapbook with special words and pictures that remind you of the person who died.

How long was your family in mourning?

What clothes did your family wear during mourning?

If anyone made special meals for your family while you were in mourning, what were the meals?

If you created a ritual after the person died, what was it?

Who helped you create the ritual?

Explain what it was like to do the ritual.

Draw a picture of how you looked while performing a ritual.

You just finished Chapter 5. Take a moment to relax and think. Focus on how your body feels. Is any part tense or uncomfortable? Notice the emotions you are experiencing. What are they? Are you feeling any strong emotions now? Name them. Find an adult to talk to, or write or draw something about your feelings. Do you want to read the next chapter now or do you want to take a break? If you take a break, find something fun or relaxing to do.

6

Grandma's Special Gift

Later that day, my dad's parents arrived from New York. It was always great spending time with Grandma and Grandpa. They talked about the funeral with my mom, aunt and uncles. Everyone was very sad. After they left, I went to my room with Grandma. She sat at the edge of my bed knitting like she always did. I sat at my desk flipping through some old comic books.

"That was your dad's desk. I bought it for him a very long time ago." She continued, "I can't believe he's gone. My precious son is gone."

"Grandma, Daddy did his homework at this desk when he was a kid."

"It seems like only yesterday your dad was a boy sitting at that desk."

Grandpa was walking up and down the hall. He seemed angry and pacing faster and faster. It was hard to understand what he was saying, partly because he still had a Brooklyn accent and partly because he was a fast talker.

He came into my doorway saying, "Hey, Buddy." He actually sounded like Dad. Though it was weird, it also felt good, reassuring almost to hear the sound of Dad's voice—something I had always taken for granted—up until now. Grandma told him to stop pacing. Grandpa looked at me, rolled his eyes and smiled. By this time he was all the way in my bedroom. Grandpa stood by my magnetic dart board. He picked up six darts. As he threw each dart, he said, "These darts are strong."

"Super strong, Grandpa."

"That's a dangerous toy," Grandma said.

"It's magnetic," Grandpa and I said at the same exact time.

"Oh, okay. I just don't want anyone else getting hurt."

Grandpa touched Grandma's shoulder and said, "No one is going to get hurt, dear." Grandpa looked around my room and noticed my ant farm. "What do you feed your ants?"

"Grandpa, I don't have to feed them. They live in a nutrient gel."

"It looks like your ants have worked hard creating those long tunnels," Grandpa said.

"Well, this is the longest day of my life. I don't know if it's the grief or the jet lag, but I'm done," Grandma said. She put down her knitting. "I want to go to sleep. We should all get to bed, including those ants. I'm sure those ants are tired from digging those tunnels."

Grandpa mumbled, "I know I won't sleep a wink."

I started to cry when I heard him say that. *I won't sleep a wink* was Dad's favorite saying when he was really tired.

"Grandma, it was strange going to sleep last night."

"What was strange about it, Alex?"

"Daddy wasn't home. It was just weird. What if I have a nightmare about Daddy?"

"Aw, Alex," she said. "Listen, a nightmare is confusing and scary. I think a nightmare can help you cope with the changes in your life. When I wake up from a nightmare I think of ways to change the ending."

"You go back into your nightmare?"

"I certainly do! Your grandma is quite brave. I just make the ending one that I like. It's a lot less scary that way. Then I go back to bed."

"Tell the kid about the time I woke up from a nightmare where a giant was chasing me. You told me to create a magical shield," Grandpa said.

"Yep, that giant could not hurt Grandpa because he went back into the dream and had a shield to protect him."

"Even though nightmares can scare you, remember your room is a safe place. Okay, I'll let you spend some time with Grandma," he said as he gave me a kiss on the cheek and went to bed.

"Grandma, I just don't feel safe. Daddy is never going to be here to protect me. Uncle Sammy is thirty minutes away. It's scary sometimes."

"Sometimes bad things happen to us. It can be very hard. Sometimes we do get scared. But we have each other and God will always be with us. God can help us to find the strength and courage we need to get through the bad times." She paused and looked at the poster on the wall, a few photos in frames, and my collection of rocks on my dresser. "You sure do have lots of rocks. Look around your room. All your things are here. Mom is in her bedroom and Debbie is sleeping right down the hall. Grandpa and I are sleeping over. If you have a dream about Daddy, good or bad, you can wake me up and we'll talk about it."

I noticed Grandma was wearing a man's watch and asked, "Grandma, are you wearing my dad's watch?"

"Yes, I am. It feels good wearing something that belonged to him. Your mom said I could wear it. If you would like it,

I can ask Mom if I can give it to you. Do you want to wear something that belonged to your dad?"

"I want his favorite T-shirt and his baseball cap," I sighed.

Grandma kept touching Dad's watch as she got up from the bed. "I'll be back in a flash," she assured me as she left my room. After a few minutes, she came back to my room and handed me Dad's baseball cap. "Sorry it took so long. Uncle Gary was on the phone. He and Aunt Jennifer are at the hotel. He called to make sure you and Debbie are okay." The cap was old and worn. It was Dad's and I loved it. I thought about him wearing it as I put it on my head.

"It's a little big," Grandma said, as she pulled it down over my eyes.

"I can fix it. It's fine," I assured her. It felt good wearing my dad's cap. "Grandma, I like talking to you."

"And I like talking to you, too. It's good to find people to talk to."

"I'm not going to talk about what happened to Dad with my friends or the kids at school. I'll just talk to my family."

"It sounds like you want to keep your dad's suicide a secret. Do you think that it is the best way to deal with what happened?"

"Grandma, the kids at school still have dads. I don't know anyone whose dad killed himself."

"That may make it hard for them to understand what you're going through."

"Grandma, they won't get it because I hardly get it myself."

"You're right. Who could possibly understand how deeply you hurt?"

"You do, Grandma. But I'm embarrassed." I started to cry so hard I thought I would never stop. Finally, I looked up at Grandma.

"What are you embarrassed about, Alex?"

"Daddy's suicide," I sobbed.

"Your dad suffered from depression. Because he had a disease in his brain, he wasn't thinking clearly. He had really poor judgment."

"It's hard to talk about, Grandma."

"Whether someone dies by suicide, homicide, AIDS, cancer, a car crash, or heart attack, it's not going to be easy to talk about. There's nothing to be embarrassed about. Adults have a hard time talking about death, no matter what the cause. I can't imagine how hard it is for a child to understand. Just talk with someone you trust, whether a friend or one of us. You can always talk with me."

"Maybe I'll talk to my teacher about Dad."

"I'm glad you have a teacher to talk with about what happened. There are a lot of people who care about you. I love you, Alex."

"I love you back, Grandma."

"Good night, sleep tight," she said as she closed the door. Grandma tried to help me understand what happened to Dad. It was hard for her because I don't think she understood it herself. Having my grandparents around always made me feel better. But they seemed different. I put my dad's baseball cap on the table next to my bed. I thought to myself, if I have a nightmare, I'll wake up and put on the baseball cap. It will be my shield.

I had lots of thoughts as I tried to sleep. I was thinking about ghosts. Was Dad a ghost in my house now? I was scared. Dozing off, I noticed the glow in the dark stars on the ceiling. I would usually stare at them until I fell asleep. But, I didn't want to see the stars. I covered my head with my pillow. As I tried to go to sleep, I heard a knock at the door and my mom's voice.

"Can I come in?"

"Sure Mom. I wasn't asleep yet."

"I see you have Dad's baseball cap."

"It's going to protect me while I sleep. It's my shield."

"You've been talking to Grandma."

"Yeah. If I see a ghost in the middle of the night it will protect me."

"Ghosts are in the movies, not in real life."

"Daddy might be a scary ghost, Mom."

"He is not a scary ghost. Daddy is in heaven."

"I guess."

"Where do you think he is now?"

"I guess he's in heaven, Mom."

"He's in heaven."

"I know, Mom. But, I want him here with me."

"He should be here with you. No matter where Daddy is, in a way he will always be a part of who you are. Some people believe we just die. I believe he's in heaven. He is safe and okay and not a scary ghost either."

"I'm tired, Mom."

"Me too."

"I just want to go to bed, Mom."

"It's been a long day. And I'm afraid that tomorrow is going to be just as long. Tomorrow is Daddy's funeral. We're going to get up early. Try to get to sleep. I love you."

"I love you too, Mom."

Alex shared his story with you. When you are ready, you can share your story with an adult. Here are some questions and activities to explore . . .

Let's Identify
Your Thoughts and Feelings

What kinds of thoughts are going through your mind right now?

What did Chapter 6 make you think about?

Has someone said or done something that reminded you of the person who died? If so, explain what it was.

Does your home feel safe? Explain your answer.

If you do not feel safe in your home, what can you do about it?

Where do you feel the safest?

With whom do you feel the safest?

Can you describe why you feel safe in this place and with this person?

If you could have one item that belonged to the person who died, what would it be?

Why would you choose this item?

If you already have something that belonged to this person, describe it.

Why does the object have a special meaning?

Where do you keep this special object?

How does the object make you feel connected to the person?

Have you had any dreams about the person who died? If so, describe your dream.

If you had a dream, was it comforting? Explain why it was or was not comforting.

If you ever had a nightmare, how did it make you feel?

What do you do to feel less scared when you wake up from a nightmare?

You just finished Chapter 6. Take a moment to relax and think. Focus on how your body feels. Is any part tense or uncomfortable? Notice the emotions you are experiencing. What are they? Are you feeling any strong emotions now? Name them. Find an adult to talk to, or write or draw something about your feelings. Do you want to read the next chapter now or do you want to take a break? If you take a break, find something fun or relaxing to do.

7

When Grief Hurts

The funeral was the saddest day of my life. Uncle Sammy and Uncle Gary talked about Dad. Grandma and Grandpa were holding each other. Mom didn't say anything. She cried the entire time. Aunt Jennifer held Debbie's hand. Debbie held onto her doll. I knew most of the people. They were nice. Dad's boss told me that my dad was a good man. His friends told me that they will miss him and how sorry they were that he died. I put a few rocks in Dad's casket, a picture of us fishing and a note. Debbie drew a picture. Mom put it in the casket with the other stuff.

Lots of people came back to our house to eat after the funeral. Debbie started once again, "Happy birthday to me, happy birthday to me . . ." She kept singing it over and over again. Usually, Debbie's singing and playing at the table didn't bother me. Today, for some reason, I couldn't stand it. A little over a week before Dad died, Debbie had a birthday party. She got dolls and coloring books. She had a Barbie cake with pink and purple icing and five magic candles that she couldn't blow out. It seems like that fun day happened months ago.

"Deb, please stop singing," I pleaded, as she kept getting louder and louder. I said, "I can't hear myself think!"

Mom dropped her fork and stared at me. Dad used to say that. I guess it reminded both of them of him because Debbie asked, "Where's Daddy?"

Mom whispered, "Debbie, remember we talked about what happened to Daddy. He's dead, sweetheart. We went to his funeral today. Daddy died."

"Daddy died?" Debbie asked.

"Yeah, Deb, he is in heaven."

"Did a monster take him away, Mommy?" Debbie asked.

"Don't be stupid, Debbie," I yelled.

Mom shot me a look of rage before explaining, "Debbie, there's no such thing as a monster."

Debbie dropped her crayons, "If I wish real hard, could I make Daddy come back?"

If it was only that easy, I thought.

"I wish Daddy was home. What time is he coming home?"

I tried to ignore her, but she really didn't get it. I was her big brother. I got it. I felt like I should explain what I knew about death. "Daddy's never coming home. No monster hurt him. We don't have the power to wish him back home, or back with us at the kitchen table. He's going to be dead forever." As I said the words it started to sink in. He was never coming home. Our breakfast, or any meal, would never be the same. No matter what time of the day it was, or what meal we ate together, he would never sit with us at the table ever again.

"I'm proud of you, Alex. Just eleven years old and so wise." Holding Debbie's hand, Mom said, "Deb, when people die, their bodies don't work anymore. Daddy's body doesn't work anymore."

"Dad's body doesn't work?" Debbie asked.

"No it doesn't. His heart stopped beating. He doesn't breathe anymore."

"How can he eat if he can't breathe?" Debbie asked.

"He can't eat, honey. When people are dead, they don't need to eat."

"Daddy loves hot dogs. Doesn't he want to eat while he's in heaven?" Debbie asked.

"I don't believe he needs to eat in heaven. But if there are hot dogs in heaven, then I'm sure your daddy will be eating one. I believe he's at peace. He doesn't need food like we do. Daddy is dead."

After Mom told Debbie that our dad was dead for what felt like the hundredth time, Deb told Mom that her stomach hurt. As Mom gently rubbed Debbie's stomach, she told her that everything was going to be okay and that God would take care of us. She explained, "Every faith is different. Some faiths believe that when people die, they go to heaven. That's what we believe. Daddy is in heaven with God. The way Daddy loved us will always be a part of who we are."

"What if someone else in our family dies?"

"That's a very scary question, Alex. Everyone dies. But, I don't know anyone who is dying," Mom said.

"Grandpa and Grandma are old. They could die."

Mom spoke in her sweetest voice. It was the voice she used when she knew I was scared about something. "You're right; they very well could die. We are all going to die one day. Lucky for us, Grandma and Grandpa are both quite healthy. Heaven can wait!"

"I'm going to draw a picture of Daddy in heaven," Deb said.

"Show me . . . I want to see it when you're done," I requested as I poured another glass of orange juice.

"Hey Mom, do you believe that Daddy can see us from heaven?"

"Alex, I don't think he watches us all the time. I believe he can see us when we need him to see us," she explained.

"What do you think heaven is like, Mom?"

"Alex, it's peaceful. Love exists in heaven. Daddy is with all the angels. He's also with our family and friends who have died. When we need to feel his presence, he'll be smiling down on us from heaven."

"I haven't seen Dad smile in a long time."

"I believe he's smiling now, Alex."

"God is in heaven. Daddy is with God," Debbie said.

Mom smiled and said, "That is what's getting me through this hard time. I believe Dad is no longer hurting inside and he's with God. He's happy in heaven. Heaven is filled with sunlight. It's peaceful." Mom looked out the kitchen window and up at the clouds. Without taking her eyes from the sky, Mom asked, "Alex, what do you think heaven looks like?"

"Mom, I think heaven is a place where people don't hurt. I think it's a place where we can see family and friends who have died. Heaven is where God lives."

As my mom kept looking up at the sky, tears rolled down her cheeks. One of her friends came over and put her arms around her.

"Mom, don't you remember what Grandpa told us after his dog, Patches, died? He said he would see him again one day in heaven."

Grandma, while on her way to the kitchen, overheard us and added, "I recently saw a picture with cats on it that had a saying, *Heaven is where all the cats we ever loved will meet us once again.*" Grandma started crying as she poured her coffee into the cup that had the words, *Best Dad in the Whole World.* "I guess heaven is filled with old friends, family, cats and dogs," Mom sighed.

"Birds too, Mommy. They just fly right up there," Debbie said.

As Grandma poured her coffee, I said, "That's Dad's coffee cup, Grandma. You're drinking from Daddy's cup. That's . . ."

"Oh my goodness. I'm so sorry. I didn't realize . . ."

Mom assured Grandma. "It's okay. It's okay. You can use his cup."

"Do you mind my using your dad's cup, Alex?"

"I don't mind. It's just, well, it's Daddy's cup. It's okay. I don't think Daddy would mind, either."

"I think your dad would probably say it's okay, too."

"I have so much to say to him. I wonder if he can hear me," I thought out loud.

Mom said, "I believe when you have something to say that you want him to hear, he will be able to hear you. What do you want to say to him, Alex?"

"I want to ask him why he killed himself."

"What do you think your dad would say to you?" Mom questioned.

"Maybe he would say he was sorry. He would say he should have stayed alive to be with me. I'm angry that he killed himself. Now, he won't be here to take me places and spend time with me. I understand he's with God, but I want him with me. It's not fair."

"It's not fair. It's totally unfair," Mom said as she handed me a book with blank pages in it. She thought a journal might be a good place to write about my thoughts and feelings. I thanked her and decided to go back to my room. After staring at the journal, I eventually decided to place it on my shelf right between my two favorite books, *James and the Giant Peach* and *Shoeless Joe & Me*.

It was hard to concentrate. There were so many people in the house. I walked back into the kitchen and noticed Mom was talking to Grandma. I wondered what Mom was going to do with Dad's cup. It really was weird seeing Grandma drink from it. Within a few minutes our next door neighbors came over. I hung up their coats. When I opened the hall closet, I moved a few coats around to make room for their heavy coats. That's when I saw it . . . Dad's coat. I just stared at it. It made me feel strange. "Mom, can I talk to you about something?"

"Anything," she said. Mom and I sat down on the couch near the warm fireplace. It reminded me of the times Dad and I roasted marshmallows.

"Mom, who lit the fireplace?"

"I did. There's a first time for everything, Alex. I have a strong feeling there will be a lot of firsts around here."

Although the room was warm, I suddenly felt cold. I felt . . . I really didn't know how I felt.

"I feel so weird."

"Is it your mind that feels strange or your body?"

"I don't know, Mom."

"Do you have a bad headache? Do you feel dizzy?"

"Mom, I've got a stomachache. Am I getting sick?"

"I don't think so. When someone we love dies, our body reacts. Do you remember when I was talking with Debbie about Daddy's death? She said that her stomach hurt."

"Yeah, that's right, Mom. I remember."

"A stomachache is a normal reaction to loss. Certain thoughts, feelings and even some behaviors will change as you grieve. I feel like I've had a non-stop headache these past few days and it's perfectly normal. It's called grief."

"Grief. Oh yeah, I heard of it, Mom."

"Grief is when your body and mind try to handle a very sad loss. You have grief reactions because of loss. Your loss is your dad's death. Everyone has different grief reactions. It's okay to have them. I sure do. I'm really, really sad."

"Me too, Mom."

"Feeling mad or having a stomachache or a headache are normal grief reactions. Sometimes when I think about your dad, I get sad and I cry. Whenever that happens I try to think of a happy memory with him. It helps me to deal with his death."

"I won't cry in front of the kids at school. They'll think I'm weird."

"It sounds like it might bother you if they have those thoughts. You can cry by yourself or cry with someone you feel safe with and can trust. You can always come to me."

"If the kids saw me cry, they might laugh."

"They might. That's because they don't understand, not because there's anything wrong with crying when someone we love dies," she explained.

"I would hit them really hard if they tease me."

"No, no, try not to act on your angry feelings. Hurting others will only hurt you worse. The old rules still apply. Grief doesn't give you the right to hurt people with your words or actions. Instead of hitting someone, can you think of something else to do if you're angry?"

"I could walk away from the kids who tease me."

"That's a great idea. See, you're understanding ways to cope. What else can you do?"

"I could tell a teacher."

"Good, very nice. I like your ideas a lot."

"I guess I could play sports. That always helps me get out my anger. I'm angry Daddy's dead. Why did he want to leave me?"

"He didn't want to leave you. He was only thinking of ending his painful feelings. I'm trying to figure it all out. Dad felt anxious all the time. He couldn't concentrate. I think he felt hopeless. Toward the end, he didn't want to talk about how he was feeling. This is so hard. I need one of your hugs." As we hugged each other I felt numb. Mom promised, "We are a family and as a family we will get through all of this."

"Mom, lately he didn't want to play ball with me. I was confused because he always played with me. The day before he died, I asked him to play ball. He didn't want to play."

"Lately, Dad didn't have an interest in anything."

"Not even me, Mom, not even me."

"He loved you. Dad was just hurting so much inside. He couldn't show you how much he loved you. Talking about him helps us to understand what he was going through."

Mom was talking about depression and brain chemicals, but I stopped listening. I just sat frozen on the couch. I kept staring out the window at the trees covered in snow. I had so many thoughts in my head. Why did he kill himself? How could he do this to me? Who is going to help me with my homework? What am I going to tell my friends? Should I still be in the school play? Who is going to take me to my baseball practice? Is Mommy going to die? I couldn't speak. I just thought and thought and thought until my head started to ache. Mom brought me back down to earth. "Are you listening to me as I'm talking to you? Is there something about Daddy that's on your mind right now? You can talk to me. I want you to talk to me."

"Mom, do you think if I had been with him, I could have kept him alive?"

"I don't think there's anything you could have done. What do you think?"

"I was his son. I should have known he was going to kill himself."

"Did you see any signs he was going to kill himself, Alex?"

"No. I guess not."

"Did he tell you he was going to shoot himself?" Mom asked.

"No, but . . ."

"But what?" Mom interrupted. "There is no way you could have read his mind. I know I couldn't. Neither could his doctor and he's trained to see the signs."

"Mom, it's unfair. Daddy left me."

"We can talk about blame and unfairness. We can talk about what we could have done or should have done. I believe God will help us find some of the answers, so we don't blame ourselves."

I didn't know what to believe. All I knew was Dad was dead. And this thing called grief, whatever it meant, was the worst feeling I had ever felt in my life.

Alex shared his story with you. When you are ready, you can share your story with an adult. Here are some questions and activities to explore . . .

Let's Identify
Your Thoughts and Feelings

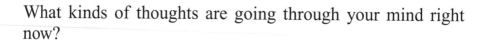

What kinds of thoughts are going through your mind right now?

What did Chapter 7 make you think about?

If you attended the funeral, describe what you saw.

If you had to explain death and suicide to someone younger than you, what would you say?

How does talking about the person who died help you to cope with your loss?

What does the death of this person mean to you?

Were you ever afraid that someone else you cared about was going to die? If so, please explain.

What happens when people die?

Where do you think the person who died is now?

If you believe that people go somewhere else after they die, what do you think it looks like?

If you could say anything you wanted to the person who died and that person could hear you, what would you say?

If you sometimes see items that belonged to the person who died, what does it feel like when you see those things?

If you got angry since the death, what was the reason?

What beliefs do you have about the suicide that are causing you to get angry?

If you ever get angry, what things do you do to deal with your anger?

What grief reactions have you noticed in your body?

On a piece of paper, draw a picture of the place in your body that hurts or feels mixed-up.

You just finished Chapter 7. Take a moment to relax and think. Focus on how your body feels. Is any part tense or uncomfortable? Notice the emotions you are experiencing. What are they? Are you feeling any strong emotions now? Name them. Find an adult to talk to, or write or draw something about your feelings. Do you want to read the next chapter now or do you want to take a break? If you take a break, find something fun or relaxing to do.

8

Catching Up with Coach

The day after the funeral Aunt Jennifer and Uncle Gary went home. Uncle Sammy went back to work. Grandma and Grandpa were staying at our house for a few weeks. Debbie and I stayed home from school. When my stomach began to growl, I knew it was lunchtime. My report on Thomas Jefferson was due that morning. My teacher told Mom I could hand it in late without any penalty. I thought about working on my science project of the galaxy. It was due next week. I just didn't want to think about Dad. I was in the kitchen trying to figure out which flavor cookie I wanted, chocolate chip or oatmeal raisin . . . so many choices! The doorbell rang.

"Can you get the door, Alex? I'm on the phone," Mom asked.

My baseball coach, Charlie, was standing outside the door with a box of pizza. He must have just got back from vacation. His face was as red as a watermelon. "Boy, do you have a sunburn, Coach Charlie!"

"Yeah, I know. You'd never know I put on sunscreen, huh? It was hot in Florida," he chuckled.

"Did you have fun, Coach? Come on in."

"I really did, Alex. Thanks for asking."

As I closed the front door behind him, he told me why he came to see me. "When I got back, I heard the news that your dad died. I'm sorry."

"Thanks, Coach. You came to my house because my dad died?" I asked, taking the pizza box out of his hands.

"Yeah. I'm sorry he died. I snuck out of school to bring you a pizza. I have to tell ya, kid, I don't have a pass."

"You don't need one, Coach."

"Oh, right! I forgot." As we stood in the foyer laughing, I realized that I hadn't laughed like that since my dad died. I needed that laugh. I felt like life was normal—as if my heart was never broken and I didn't have a ton of questions. All of a sudden I started to feel guilty. My dad just died. He died by suicide and I was laughing. I didn't like the way I felt. My stomach was growling. Coach, pointing to it, asked, "Is there a bear cub in there?"

"Yeah, he's hibernating, Coach."

Mom got off the phone and said, "Charlie, what a nice surprise! And you brought pizza. What a dear. Thank you. Please, come in and eat." While Mom poured our drinks and set the table, Coach Charlie told her how sorry he was about what happened to my dad. Mom thanked him and smiled, as she opened the box of pizza. Mom handed both of us a paper plate. "Gentlemen, dig in! If you'll excuse me, I have to make a few phone calls." Mom walked up the stairs, leaving me and Coach alone.

"Hey, kid, why does a round pizza come in a square box?" Coach Charlie asked.

"I have no idea."

"Me either. Who cares, right? Let's eat!" Coach laughed. We ate pizza and drank root beer. After I told Coach about what happened to my dad, I had to ask a very big question. Since Dad had always taken me to baseball practice, I was afraid I might not be a part of the team anymore. "Coach, my dad always took me to the games. Who's going to take me to my practice and games now?"

"Well," Coach responded, "If your Mom says it's okay, I can take you. Would you like that?"

"Yeah. I know we have plenty of time. But it was on my mind. Thanks, Coach."

"Sure. You don't have to worry about missing any of your practices or games."

"I can't believe my dad won't be at my games anymore. I keep thinking about that."

He paused for a second, "I'm sure you have a lot on your mind these days, Alex."

"I'm also thinking about the last time I saw my dad."

"Where was he?"

"He was at the kitchen table. He usually drank coffee and read the paper. That morning, he wasn't doing either one. I should have known something was wrong. I should have known he was going to kill himself."

"It sounds like you blame yourself."

"I didn't get the chance to say goodbye to my dad."

"Did he say goodbye to you?"

"No." I could feel the tears rising up on the inside. "Coach, I was late for the bus and ran out of the house."

"I hear you. You're upset with yourself for not saying goodbye to him."

"I just wish I would have said goodbye."

"Alex, you can always say goodbye."

"No way, Coach. If the person is dead, it's too late to say goodbye."

"You could write your dad a goodbye letter. Write down whatever it is you need to say to him. Keep it in a special place. Read it whenever you want. I believe when someone we care about dies, we say goodbye to what we shared with them. But your dad will always be a part of you."

"But I didn't say goodbye."

Very slowly, Coach repeated himself, "You can always say goodbye."

"I miss him. I can't believe he's dead. He won't be at my games, Coach."

"He was always at your games. This is a tough break. I'm sorry. Remember when we won last year's season opener? Your dad jumped up and down and fell over. He didn't hurt himself, but boy was that funny."

"Coach, that was hysterical. I never saw my dad so happy. He had his camcorder in one hand and a hot dog in the other."

"Good memories, kid. That's what you have to hold onto. I never told you this, but when my dad died a few years ago, I made a list of all the favorite memories I shared with him. I still have the list to this day."

"Your dad died, too?"

"Yeah, he died. Boy, do I miss him. Although the world goes on, there is hardly a day in my life when I don't think about him or miss him." We both finished our last bites of pizza. "Some things will change. Lots of things are still going to be the same as they always were. You still go to school. You still read books you enjoy. You still play baseball. You still have people who love you. You still have your friends on the team."

"Coach, what do you think I should tell my friends on the team if they ask why my dad died?"

"The question 'Why?' is a very difficult question to answer. You are just learning the 'whys' yourself. Share what you know and only if you want to."

"What if some of the kids at school find out he died by suicide and stare at me? I hate teasing."

"That might make you feel uncomfortable. Every child is different. Some might stare at you. Some kids might avoid you. Some kids may say they're sorry he died. Your friends may help you catch up with homework. Your close friends will be glad to see you back at school."

"Do you think kids at school will treat me differently? I don't want them to act weird or anything."

"I don't know what they will do. We could talk about it if you like."

"Coach, I guess I'll find out sooner or later. I just wasn't ready for my dad to die right now. No matter how hard you want someone to come alive again, when they're dead, they're dead!"

"It was a very sad thing that happened. Has anyone you've known died before, Alex?"

"No, not a person. My cat, Jackson, died last year. My Grandpa's dog died too."

"It's sad when pets die. Tell me more about how you felt when Jackson died."

"I thought I was to blame. I even thought I could have done something to keep him alive. I cried. I miss him. The day Jackson died, my friend, Wendy, asked me to come to her house for lunch. I told her I wasn't hungry even though I was. She had a cat, Gracie, and I didn't feel like seeing her cat."

"What do you think would have happened if you went to Wendy's house?"

"Gracie would have rubbed against my leg. I like her cat. It would have been hard to play with the cat when I was sad about my own cat dying."

"Did you ever go back to your friend's house?"

"After a couple of weeks. I even played with Gracie. When I got home, I took a photo of Jackson out of an album and put it in a frame on my desk. I kept his stuffed mouse I used to dip with catnip. He'd swat at it and throw it in the air. Sometimes, it even hit the ceiling."

"You have some happy memories of your cat."

"I guess I do. All I know for sure is I still miss him. Now, I miss Dad."

"Let's go for a walk and talk about it." Coach put his arm around my shoulders. We went for a long walk even though it was freezing. Having him to talk to was important to me. I think that he cared about me. Talking to people I trusted made me feel better. I don't think they have all the answers. It felt good knowing they were trying to understand how I felt.

As we walked back to the house, I blurted out, "Coach, my dad died in the basement and ever since, I'm afraid to go down there."

"What are you afraid of?"

"I know it's cleaned up. It would feel weird to see the place where he died."

"Weird?"

"Yeah. He died down there."

"Would it help if the first time you go into the basement, your mom went with you?"

"Maybe."

"In time, you will probably be less afraid to go into the basement by yourself. I can see how going to the place where your dad died by suicide could be upsetting. Ask your mom to go with you when you need to go into the basement, until you feel safe enough to go down there on your own."

"I'm not in any hurry, Coach."

"There's no rush." Coach told me that he had to get back to school or he would get suspended. He said, "The principal will probably make me clean the school, too, if I don't hurry. Oh wait one minute. I almost forgot." He ran over to his car and came back and handed me a book. He said, "*Honus & Me*. It's about baseball. Whenever I'm feeling sad, I read books about things I enjoy doing. I thought this might help you out."

"Thanks, Coach."

"Well, I hope you liked the pizza. Like I said, if you ever need someone to talk to, I'm here for you."

When Coach left, I went to my room. I kept lined paper and pens in my desk drawer. The top of my desk was covered with schoolbooks, a test paper my mom had to sign, two empty cans of soda and two dead batteries. My batteries always seemed to be dead. 'The batteries are dead!' I would say out loud. But batteries don't die, people do. I threw the batteries into the wastebasket. I sat at my large, wooden desk that was my dad's desk when he was a kid. I wondered if he kept his papers and pens in the same drawer as I did. He told me that he kept his gyroscope in the bottom drawer. I always kept mine on the shelf. I got up from the desk. I picked up my gyroscope and string and put it in the bottom drawer, just like the way my dad did. I then wrote a list of good things I remembered about him. When I was done with my list, I took out another sheet of paper from the drawer and wrote Dad a letter.

Dear Daddy,

I'm remembering all the times we shared together. I think you were the best Dad in the whole world. I'm sad you're dead. I wish you hadn't killed yourself. I don't know why you did it. We talked about everything. But for some strange reason, we never talked about you ever leaving me. We said so much to one another. I have been thinking about our conversations. I can still hear your voice talking to me. I said a lot to you, too. I said, thank you for helping me with my homework. I told you thanks for making me feel like the smartest kid in the world. I hope you knew how much I appreciated you. The problem is, I have been thinking about the things I said to you. But I didn't say goodbye, and that hurts so much. Someone close to me told me that you can always say goodbye. So, goodbye, Dad. Goodbye.

Love,

Alex

Alex shared his story with you. When you are ready, you can share your story with an adult. Here are some questions and activities to explore . . .

Let's Identify Your Thoughts and Feelings

What kinds of thoughts are going through your mind right now?

What did Chapter 8 make you think about?

Is there anything the person who died did for you that another person is now doing?

What is your favorite memory of the person who died?

If you are staying away from a place that reminds you of this person's death, describe the place.

What would happen if you went to this place?

What was your biggest fear after this person died?

How did you cope with your fear?

Write a list of things people said to you since the death that were helpful.

People usually mean well, but they don't always say things that seem nice or helpful. What were some things people said to you that made you feel worse/more confused/angry instead of better?

If you did not have a chance to say goodbye, write a goodbye letter.

You just finished Chapter 8. Take a moment to relax and think. Focus on how your body feels. Is any part tense or uncomfortable? Notice the emotions you are experiencing. What are they? Are you feeling any strong emotions now? Name them. Find an adult to talk to, or write or draw something about your feelings. Do you want to read the next chapter now or do you want to take a break? If you take a break, find something fun or relaxing to do.

9

One Month Later

As I walked into the kitchen for some chocolate milk, I overheard Mom on the phone. She was talking to someone about Dad. "It's been one month. Where did the time fly? I can't believe he's been gone a whole month. We're doing fine. The kids are fine. Sure, I'll mention bereavement counseling with the kids and see what they say . . . I'll let you know. It might be a good idea." Mom hung up the phone and said, "Hey, Alex. That was my friend, Chris. She told me about a bereavement counselor she went to a few years ago."

"What's a bereavement counselor?"

Mom explained, "Sometimes families go to bereavement counselors to help them cope after someone dies."

"We're coping."

"I think we are, too. But, it's hard being bereaved."

"Huh?"

"Bereaved. When people experience a loss of someone close to them, they become bereaved. They are really sad because someone they cared about, died. You're sad because Dad died."

"I don't need a counselor. I have you."

"Yes, you do have me and I have you. I think that a counselor can help both of us. A bereavement counselor is someone who could help us cope with daddy's death. You heard Grandma say, 'We lost him.' You also heard Grandpa say, 'He was taken from us.' Right?"

"Right, Mom. I heard them say that."

"These words mean the same thing—to be bereaved."

"Mom, I don't need any help. I'm fine."

"You are doing fine. You've been a big help to me this past month."

"And you've been a big help to me. Mom, I'm okay."

"Your dad's death was sudden. Chris was telling me that bereavement counselors can help families after a suicide."

"We don't need help, Mom."

"When people are dealing with a suicide, like we are, counseling can help them cope with grief. We talked about grief after Daddy died. It's when your body reacts to a loss. In the past month, you have had a few stomachaches and headaches."

"I had a bad stomachache the other day."

"That's normal, Alex."

"I don't want to talk to a stranger about my feelings."

"I can understand that. Bereavement counselors are not for everyone. They can help, especially when grief hurts so much." She continued, "Most people don't need counselors. They have friends, relatives, and their faith to help them when their grief becomes painful."

"We have those things, Mom."

"Yes, we do. But I need more help."

"It's only been a month, Mom. It's going to be okay."

"I think seeing a bereavement counselor can help me cope with your dad's suicide. I want to go. I want to make sure you and Debbie are okay."

"We're okay, Mom. We don't have to go. Deb and I don't need any help."

"Debbie woke up in the middle of the night. She was screaming. I need to talk to a bereavement counselor. Let's just go once and see if it's for us."

"Okay, Mom. If Debbie needs it. I guess we can try it. Sometimes it hurts to talk about Daddy. Sometimes I want to change the way I feel, Mom. I want to go back to the way I felt before he died."

"I want to go back in time too. We can't actually do that. What we can do is talk about the past, remember your dad, and share our grief. We have all kinds of feelings like being numb, confused, lonely, sad and angry."

"I'm really angry about what happened. I'm confused, too, Mom."

"Alex, I've decided that I'm going to a support group."

"A support group?"

"Yeah, a support group. A group of people bereaved by suicide meet to talk about their feelings. I think that might help me deal with my grief. When we grieve, our mind reacts. We have different thoughts and emotions," she said.

Before she explained anything more, I interrupted, "Mom, why do I feel numb?"

"Being numb is a normal grief reaction. There are ways to cope with what you're going through." Mom explained that I could listen to my favorite music, I could talk to God, and I could always talk with her. Together, we would work it out.

"Mom, I think about Dad all the time. I think of him when I watch TV. I think of him when I'm playing in the snow. I think of him when I eat breakfast. I think of him so much."

"I do the same thing, Alex. There are so many reminders."

"Mom, I think I should have done something to save him."

She was quick to respond, "What do you think you should have done?"

"I should have talked to him before I went to school."

"About what?"

"About anything. I should have stayed home that day. Didn't he seem happier than usual?"

"I don't know. Maybe. You know, as I think about it, Daddy did seem happier than usual that morning."

"Mom, if I stayed home, he wouldn't have died. I did the wrong thing."

"Wrong thing?"

"Mom, I made a big mistake. I should have stayed home."

"It sounds like you blame yourself for his suicide."

"I do."

"You had no idea he was going to kill himself. I don't think you did the wrong thing at all. You didn't know he intended to kill himself on that day. I didn't either."

"I blame myself, Mom."

"No one is to blame."

"Mom, I think you should have known, too. Why didn't you know he was going to kill himself?"

"I didn't know. I didn't see the signs. I never thought he would kill himself."

"I went to school. I shouldn't have left you and Daddy alone."

"When you left for school, you intended to do what you do everyday, Monday through Friday. You're a child.

Children go to school. If you were home, nothing would have changed."

"Something could have changed. But we'll never know, Mom."

"Dad might have waited for another day. Or, he might have gone someplace else. I was home with him and he still killed himself. There was no way you could predict that he was going to take his life while you were at school."

"But he did kill himself while I was at school, Mom. Now, he's dead. Things would have turned out differently if I had stayed home. I don't know if I can ever forgive him for what he did to me."

"He never should have taken his life. He never should have done this to you. It was a big mistake. I can't believe he did it."

"I'm trying to forgive him for leaving me, Mom."

"I forgive him. I'm not ready to be angry with him. I'm more disappointed in his act, the suicide, but not at him."

"He shouldn't be dead."

"No, he shouldn't."

"Mom, I wrote Dad a letter."

"You did? What did you say?"

"I wrote in the letter that I missed him. I can't believe he killed himself, Mom."

"I can't believe it, either. What a huge mistake he made."

"It was the biggest mistake he could ever make, Mom."

"It sure was. I feel like I'm in a fog. I can't tell you enough how much I love you."

"I love you too, Mom."

"Daddy loves you, too, Alex."

"Then why did he kill himself?"

"I don't think I will ever have all the answers. But, that doesn't mean you should ever stop asking questions."

*Alex shared his story with you. When you are ready,
you can share your story with an adult. Here are some
questions and activities to explore . . .*

Let's Identify Your Thoughts and Feelings

What kinds of thoughts are going through your mind right now?

What did Chapter 9 make you think about?

Did you ever feel numb, confused, or angry after the person died?

What do you do to help you with these feelings?

Why do you think Alex was having difficulty handling the death of his father?

If your family members talked about the death, did they say anything that may have scared or confused you?

If you blame yourself or someone else for the person's death, explain why you feel this way.

Describe the part of your experience that you once thought you would never tell anyone about.

What is one question you want answered today concerning grief and bereavement?

You just finished Chapter 9. Take a moment to relax and think. Focus on how your body feels. Is any part tense or uncomfortable? Notice the emotions you are experiencing. What are they? Are you feeling any strong emotions now? Name them. Find an adult to talk to, or write or draw something about your feelings. Do you want to read the next chapter now or do you want to take a break? If you take a break, find something fun or relaxing to do.

10

Six Months Later

I may sound brave by writing my story. When I think back to the day my dad killed himself, I was scared, shocked, terrified actually. It's been six months since my dad died. Around the time of his death, I didn't understand everything that was going on. I didn't know whether or not we were still a family. Mom assured me that we were even though Dad was dead. It felt weird and uncomfortable without him in the house and in my life.

I like to wear Dad's T-shirt and baseball cap. It feels good wearing stuff that belonged to him. I have the letter I wrote to him after he died. I let Mom and Grandma read the letter. All three of us talked about it. Grandma told me stories about when Dad was a little boy. She gave me a photo album with pictures of him as a kid. It was great to see him and my uncles as little boys hanging out and having fun. Grandma told me I looked like my dad in one of the pictures—that was pretty cool. That's the one I took out of the album. I keep it on my

desk in my room. I like spending time looking at the album
and all of the pictures of my dad.

I visited my Uncle Sammy's house a few times since Dad
died. Uncle Sammy put away all the pictures that had Dad in
them. He won't go to the cemetery. Mom told me he's coping
by not looking at the photos or visiting Dad's grave. I know
that my dad will never be completely gone. He's dead, but I
still feel connected to him.

On my birthday, Mom gave me a telescope. On the card
she wrote, Love, Mom and Dad. I know he's in heaven, but
seeing the word, *Dad*, on the card made me feel close to him.
Knowing that he's in heaven helps me deal with it. Sometimes
I actually feel like he's in some of the same places I am. I know
that sounds strange, but I feel like he's watching over me
whenever I need him—like a special guardian angel.

A few times, I dreamed about Dad and the way things
were when he was alive. Sometimes, it feels so real. Mom
says he comes to me in my dreams as a sign—a special way of
communicating with me.

Going back to school wasn't that big of a deal. The first
day back at school, I couldn't stop wondering if my friends
were talking about me. I had trouble focusing. My teachers
helped me. No one at school said anything stupid. Two friends
said they were sorry my dad died.

I missed my dad at different shows and events at school.
Mom and Uncle Sammy came to every event. That helped
make things a little easier. Even though my dad wasn't there,
I think he somehow knows I won awards and did well in plays.
He's proud of me. If I get a good grade, win a game, or just
want to tell my dad something, I tell him.

I pray looking out of my window at night and once I'm
finished talking to God, I save time for Dad. Sometimes, in the
morning when I run for the bus, I look up at the sky and talk
to Dad. If anyone heard me they would think I was having

a real conversation. I also talk to his picture. He can hear me. It feels good, like a relief, so why not talk to him? Grandpa once said to me, "When your dad starts answering you back, then you got issues. Until then, keep talking."

Mom went to a bereavement counselor, Lori Beth, to talk about Dad. She then brought me and Debbie to meet her. Sometimes I would see her by myself. Debbie and I also went to a children's bereavement support group. The first time my family went to see Lori Beth, we sat down on a huge leather couch. Before she could say a word, Mom said, "Lori Beth, this is so hard. I just want to make sure my kids are okay."

"I'll be okay, Mom," I said.

"Me too, Mommy!" Debbie exclaimed.

Mom looked at me and Debbie and said, "I'm really sad Daddy died. I just need to let all my feelings out. I couldn't get through this without you both." Mom explained to Lori Beth how having us around always makes her happy. "They are my pride and joy."

Lori Beth smiled saying, "I can see your children bring you comfort. You have been through a difficult time."

Mom told her what happened to Dad. She was kind to Mom. I liked her right away. She reminded me of a teacher because she wanted to teach us and at the same time listen to us. She asked Mom about the day Dad died. She explained that grief counseling was about support and education. We talked about when we would meet and the purpose of those meetings. She told us what to expect each time we met. Whatever we talked about would be confidential. Sessions with her were like becoming a member of a different kind of club . . . one where every member had experienced a death of someone in their life. She told us there would be rules to our sessions. She made the state laws for her profession and practice understandable, even for Debbie. She would have to tell officials if we ever wanted to hurt ourselves or anyone else. I was glad she didn't ask me questions about Dad's suicide right away. It was hard to talk about. Lori Beth would ask me about school, my favorite sports, music, and my assemblies. She and Deb talked about Deb's favorite colors and toys.

The best part about the counseling was that I didn't have to answer every question. I could answer the questions I felt most comfortable answering. Before I knew it, I was telling her all about him and what happened. I even made a collage. I cut out pictures of things from magazines that reminded me of Dad. I glued them to a large piece of paper. I found a picture of a wooden desk, a coffee cup, a donut and a fishing pole. I also found a picture of a baseball cap, a sports car, a TV, and Chinese food. After each meeting, I would go home with a project. Each project made me feel close to my dad. I missed him a lot.

One time, Lori Beth had a cool idea. She wanted me to draw a picture of a time machine. I could go back to any time when Dad was alive and pick a day that I'd spent with him. "Lori Beth, I just read a book where someone discovered a hologram projector chip."

"What's that?"

"It's a chip that allows people with computers to get images from the past and project them anywhere they wanted for a short period."

"Alex, that's cool."

"Can I change your assignment?"

"Sure."

"I want to imagine that I'm using a hologram projector chip that's been hooked up to my laptop."

"Wow, Alex. I wish they really had chips like that."

"I keep thinking about the morning my dad died. If I had a hologram projector chip, it would bring me back in time to the morning he died. This time, I would be late. I would miss the bus. I would make up a story."

"Alex, would you like to tell me about your story?"

"I don't know. I would just make up a story."

"Can you give me an idea about your story?"

"I would tell Mom and Dad that I had a headache. I would stay home."

"Okay," Lori Beth said.

"I would sit at the table. I would tell Dad how much I needed him."

"Needed him?"

"Oh yeah. I would ask him to help me study. I would ask him to help me practice for my assembly. I wouldn't leave him alone."

"Uh-huh."

"Whether I talked about baseball or my rock collection, I would do everything I could to let him know I loved him—that I needed him."

"Do you think that by staying by his side all day, you could have prevented his death?" Lori Beth asked.

"Everyone in my family told me there was nothing I could do even if I was home with him. I just think I could have saved him."

"It sounds like you blame yourself."

"I should have known he was going to kill himself."

"Alex, it must be hard feeling like you could have done something."

"Yeah, I could have stopped him. I just didn't know he was going to do it."

"Even though you didn't know, it seems like you feel guilty about not knowing."

"Lori Beth, if I knew, I would have stopped him from killing himself. I loved him so much. I made a mistake."

"I get what you're saying. I think it was your dad that made the mistake. Sometimes no matter what we do, when people want to end their lives, nothing will stop them. That doesn't mean people can't prevent a suicide. They can, especially when they get the person professional help."

"My dad was going to a doctor for help. Dad had a gun. He used it instead of calling his doctor."

"So, would you say that he was thinking clearly?"

"No way!"

"Why do you think he killed himself?"

"I don't know why my dad's dead. I don't know why he would kill himself."

"Do you have any guesses about why?"

"He was depressed. My mom said his brain chemicals were not working right."

"In reality you had no idea your dad was going to die of suicide. You got on the school bus."

"Yeah, I left him at home and he killed himself."

"Was your intention to go to school or to leave your father so he could end his life?"

"To go to school. I wish I had a projector chip that would allow me to go back in time. I just feel like I could have stopped him and I didn't."

"It must be hard for you to feel that way."

"I let him down."

"Tell me about how you let him down."

"I went to school instead of staying home. Don't you get it?"

"I get it. Are you angry with yourself for not staying home?"

"Yeah, I should have stayed home."

"Your feelings are important to me. It's okay to be angry."

"I should never have gone to school that day, Lori Beth."

"You're a child. Children go to school."

"I didn't do the right thing. If I was home he wouldn't have killed himself."

"Was that your job? Did someone tell you that you were supposed to stay home from school?"

"No . . ."

"Was your mom home with him?"

"Yeah. My mom should have saved him. I loved him so much. My mom should have saved him," I yelled, as I began banging my fist on the table.

"Are you trying to let me know you're angry with your mom for not saving your dad?"

"Yeah. It was her fault."

"Did she know he was going to kill himself that day?"

"No. She didn't know."

"Hmm," Lori Beth thought out loud.

"Maybe, I let her down because I didn't know. I should have known."

"How should you have known?"

"I don't know. I'm so mixed up."

"This must feel confusing."

"Yeah, I guess. I don't know."

"What do you know?"

"I know I'm mad because my dad died. I know I miss him. I know I'm sad. It hurts so much."

"And I know you loved your Dad."

Barely able to speak I mumbled, "And . . . I know he loved me back."

Alex shared his story with you. When you are ready, you can share your story with an adult. Here are some questions and activities to explore . . .

Let's Identify
Your Thoughts and Feelings

What kinds of thoughts are going through your mind right
now?

What did Chapter 10 make you think about?

How long has it been since your person died?

Have you avoided doing something that reminds you of the person who died?

Do you still feel connected to the person who died? If so, describe how you still feel connected.

If you have had any problems at school, with your friends or family since your loss, what were the problems?

Did you ever wish for something and regret it later? What was it?

If you were magically granted three wishes, what would you wish?

If you could go back in time to be with the person who died, which day would you choose?

What made you chose this particular day?

What questions do you still have about what happened?

Are you doing anything now that would make the person who died proud of you?

Create a memory box out of a shoe box, coffee can, or plastic storage container. Decorate your memory box with ribbon, wrapping paper, sparkle glue, buttons, pictures from magazines, and crayons. Write your loved one's name on the box and fill it with things that remind you of him or her. You can fill it with things like photos, jewelry, vacation souvenirs, or ticket stubs.

Make a collage. First get a piece of oak tag or large sheet of paper. Cut out pictures from magazines of things that remind you of the person who died. Place some glue on the back of each picture and place them on the oak tag or paper.

You just finished Chapter 10. Take a moment to relax and think. Focus on how your body feels. Is any part tense or uncomfortable? Notice the emotions you are experiencing. What are they? Are you feeling any strong emotions now? Name them. Find an adult to talk to, or write or draw something about your feelings. Do you want to read the next chapter now or do you want to take a break? If you take a break, find something fun or relaxing to do.

11

One Year Anniversary

After a year, I still miss my dad very much. Coach kept his word. He drove me to each practice and game. I miss the routine Dad and I had on our way to the games. I'm reminded he's dead when I pass the diner. Dad would get a cup of coffee. I lived for the apple juice and jelly donuts—two to be exact. It wasn't a ball game if I didn't end up gushing some of the jelly on my shirt. To this day, I can't eat a jelly donut. I avoid them, especially before a game. Last week, I realized Dad was gone. I looked up into the stands. Mom, Deb, and Uncle Sammy were there, smiling and cheering for me. I smiled. I waved. I missed my dad.

Today, I'm not afraid to ask questions. I ask questions about heaven and God. I ask questions about the way I feel. I ask questions about suicide. Although my mom has explained depression to me, I still ask the same question. *Why did my dad kill himself?*

On the anniversary of my dad's death, my mom's best friend gave her a piece of jewelry. She had it made with my dad's face etched on it. It's in the shape of a heart. She never takes it off. Mom gave me some of my dad's things. I was glad that she didn't throw everything away because he died. Mom told me that even though he was dead, we would keep lots of his stuff. She gave some things to charity, Debbie, Grandma and Grandpa, Uncle Gary and Uncle Sammy. She always asked me if I wanted something that belonged to him before she gave it away. Dad's things were everywhere. Whenever I turned around, I would see something that belonged to him.

My sister and I went to a bereavement support group for kids. The group met for eight weeks. The group helped me because I felt like I wasn't alone. The other kids felt some of the same feelings I did. I had a chance to talk about all the feelings that I had pushed way down inside of me. I got to hear how other kids dealt with stuff after their loved ones died and that really helped me. We made memory boxes and played games and created projects that helped me to get out my feelings of anger and loneliness and sadness and fear. I was able to understand what I was feeling. I was able to put these feelings into words.

I didn't know what to expect before I got there, but it wasn't anything like I thought it would be. The Center was great. There were pictures and quilts that different kids had made over the years. There were rooms for all the different age groups and each room had chairs and bean bags and cushions, so we could sit wherever we wanted. There were a lot of games and toys around that we could play with before or after the group meetings. There was an arts and crafts room with all kinds of stuff to do and a high energy room where we could just go when we needed to let off some steam.

Debbie was with the younger kids. I had a group with kids my own age. Mom had her own group with other parents who brought their children to the Center. Everyone who worked at the Center were really friendly. I felt like it was a safe place for me and Debbie and my mom to come to. I met a girl who wore her mother's gold necklace. Her dad killed her mom. She had to live with her aunt and uncle. Wearing her mom's necklace made her feel closer to her mom. Her mom's necklace, like my dad's baseball cap, made us feel close to our parents. Lots of the kids talked about having things that belonged to the people who died. I stayed friends with some of the kids from group. I still talk to them about my dad. We understand and are there for each other.

Alex shared his story with you. When you are ready, you can share your story with an adult. Here are some questions and activities to explore . . .

Let's Identify
Your Thoughts and Feelings

What kinds of thoughts are going through your mind right now?

What did Chapter 11 make you think about?

You feel sad when . . .

You miss the person most when . . .

What three questions do you still have about death?

What three questions do you still have about suicide?

What three questions do you still have about grief?

If anyone threw away or gave away your loved one's belongings, what was the experience like for you?

List some of the biggest changes in your life since the death.

If you could be a character in this book, who would you choose to be? Why did you choose that character?

If you could actually go into this story and meet Alex and other characters, what would you do once you were in the story?

If Alex were your pen pal and you had the opportunity to write him a letter, what would you say to him? Write about what's going on in your life right now.

You just finished Chapter 11. Take a moment to relax and think. Focus on how your body feels. Is any part tense or uncomfortable? Notice the emotions you are experiencing. What are they? Are you feeling any strong emotions now? Name them. Find an adult to talk to, or write or draw something about your feelings. Do you want to read the next chapter now or do you want to take a break? If you take a break, find something fun or relaxing to do.

12

Five Years Later

I'm now a sophomore in high school. Most of my friends don't even know what happened to my dad. I just want to fit in. I think most kids don't really get it. How could they? Mostly everyone I know has both a mom and a dad. Though I had a lot of problems in school after my dad died, my grades were good. I want to go away to college in two years. I told Mom I'm bringing Dad's chair with me to my dorm room. She couldn't understand why I want to bring an old worn out chair with me. I couldn't explain it. I just wanted it.

Sometimes I have great days. Sometimes I have terrible days. I cope with the rough days by playing sports or listening to music. My dad died 1,825 days ago. But, who's counting? Some days go really fast. Other days go really slow because something reminds me of Dad's death.

One time, Uncle Sammy drove me to a restaurant. I felt weird sitting in the front seat next to him. I felt shaky just like I did the day, five years ago, when he picked me up from school. At the restaurant, I told him what it was like for me to sit in his truck. I was upset. He said sometimes he feels the same way. Uncle Sammy explained that we had a traumatic experience. Sometimes we would be reminded of that terrible day five years ago.

Uncle Sammy explained that certain situations, like reminders of dad, make us react. What causes us to react is called a "trigger." Certain triggers can make me feel angry, numb, or shaky. I told him that the first time I went into the basement after my dad died, I panicked. I ran back up the stairs. There were times when I was in the basement, I couldn't stop thinking about how my dad killed himself down there. Uncle Sammy talked to me about my feelings. I felt scared every time I passed where he shot himself. My uncle helped me to see that it's okay to be scared. I felt frustrated. A part of me wanted to hang out in the basement. Another part of me wanted to stay far away from the place where he died. I felt nervous about it. Uncle Sammy didn't think I was being silly. He helped me to accept that the basement was where my dad died.

We talked about how situations and triggers can make me respond in a certain way. He explained that I should focus on my memories, feelings, thoughts and actions. My uncle made me see that I couldn't avoid the basement forever. He explained that if I avoid certain situations then I should focus on the consequences and how I feel by avoiding them.

After talking about what I was afraid of, we figured out that there was nothing in the basement that could hurt me. The basement looked exactly as it did before my dad died. My uncle told me that whenever I go into the basement, I should try to think about the times Dad and I would play ping pong down there—the happy times. My uncle said he was working on controlling his own triggers.

Since our talk, I have figured out more ways to distract myself when a trigger tries to get the best of me. To deal with triggers, I sometimes think about rocks and fossils my dad and I collected. I know it may sound strange, but thinking about rocks actually helps me feel better.

On those days when Uncle Sammy will be driving me somewhere, I come up with a strategy about what I will do if I get anxious in the truck. When I get anxious, my whole body gets hot. I feel dizzy. I feel nervous. I can't relax. I told my uncle that I want to ride in his truck and go places with him, but sometimes I can't stop thinking of the day he picked me up from school and told me Dad was dead. My uncle said that I should come up with something I could say to myself when I feel anxious in the truck. I came up with, *This is tough, but I will survive.* You know what? It has helped me whenever I felt anxious.

For years, Uncle Sammy wouldn't visit Dad's grave. He also put away all of Dad's photos in his house. We talked about how it took him five years to finally take out the photos and place them around the house. He also recently visited Dad's grave and plans on going again. He told me how he has to learn how to live without his brother, just like I have to learn to live without my dad. I can't change what happened. I try to remember all the good times.

When I think that five years have gone by, I just can't believe it. It seems unreal. I learned a lot about grief in the past five years. It was hard. I had to adjust and learn new skills in dealing with the tough times, especially the firsts. There were a lot of firsts after my dad died. I remember my twelfth birthday party without my dad pretending to blow out the candles on my cake. I remember the first Thanksgiving without him cutting the turkey. I remember the first vacation without him sitting next to me on the plane.

Here it is five years later; I have gone forward with my life. I have not forgotten my dad. I have accepted that he's dead. I have forgiven him for ending his life. Mom says that our memories are God's gift to us. I'm thankful for many things. I'm thankful for my family. My dad is with me every single day. I think many of the firsts are over, but if, and when, something new happens again, I'll just think of him going through it with me. I know that my dad cared for our family, despite the way he died—you can always say goodbye.

Alex shared his story with you. When you are ready, you can share your story with an adult. Here are some questions and activities to explore . . .

Let's Identify Your Thoughts and Feelings

What kinds of thoughts are going through your mind right now?

What did Chapter 12 make you think about?

Have you accepted that your person is dead?

Have you forgiven the person for taking his or her life? Explain.

If you could change two things about your life, what would the two things be?

List five things you are thankful for.

Close your eyes and see yourself five years from now. What do you see?

You are reminded of the person who died whenever you . . .

see:

hear:

touch:

smell:

taste:

imagine:

When you experience a trigger, what do you think about to help you feel better?

You just finished Chapter 12, the last chapter. There is still one last activity. It's time to write your very own book report about *But I Didn't Say Goodbye*. You can use sheets of paper or your computer for this activity.

My First Name is . . .

I am _____ years old.

This story was about . . .

The main characters were . . .

I especially liked the character, _____ because

Explain what happened in the beginning of the story.

Explain what happened in the middle of the story.

Explain what happened in the end of the story.

The main idea of the story was . . .

The main problem in the story was . . .

My favorite scene was . . .

At the end of the story . . .

Resources

A Statement of Suicide Loss Rights

1. We have the right to a grief that is complex, chronic, and disabling. Death is a normal life crisis; suicide is the ultimate abnormal life crisis.
2. We have the right to be free of stigma. In our society suicide has a negative connotation. This afflicts us as it did those we lost.
3. We have the right to be angry about our loss and to be able to express it appropriately toward the one we have lost or ourselves.
4. We have the right to feel responsible for things we did or did not do in relation to our loss. We may or may not come to feel differently.
5. We have the right to grieve in a manner and timeframe that works best for us. We don't have to "get over it."

6. We have the right to know "why." All who grieve yearn for the one lost. We also seek to understand what happened.
7. We have the right to regard our lost loved one as a victim. Suicide is the outcome of debilitation; it is not a choice or a decision.
8. We have the right to cooperation from police and the health care community if we seek information on how our loss came about.
9. We have the right to the truth about our loss. We should have access to information as early as possible, if we need it.
10. We have the right to know that we are not by definition candidates for psychotherapy or counseling, or that we must "get help."
11. We have the right to channel our experience to aid the suicidal or other suicide grievers or to help others better understand either group.
12. We have the right to never be as we were before. Other ends to grief do not apply to us. We survive, but we do not "heal."

Books for Children

Cammarota, D. (2001). *Someone I Loved Died by Suicide: A Story for Child Survivors and Those Who Care for Them.* Grief Guidance, Inc.

Cerza Kolf, J. (2002). *Standing in The Shadows.* Baker.

The Dougy Center. (2001). *After a Suicide: A Workbook for Grieving Kids.* The Dougy Center.

Goldman, L. (2006). *Children Also Grieve: Talking About Death and Healing.* Jessica Kingsley Publishers.

Grollman, E. & Johnson, J. (2001). *A Child's Book About Death.* Centering Corporation.

Jaffe, S.E. (2008). *For the Grieving Child: An Activities Manual.* Acme Bookbinding Company.

Leeuwenburgh, E. & Goldring, E. (2008). *Why Did You Die?: Activities to Help Children Cope with Grief and Loss.* New Harbinger Publications.

Loehr, C.A. (2006). *My Uncle Keith Died.* Trafford Publishing.

Requarth, M. (2006). *After a Parent's Suicide: Helping Children Heal.* Healing Hearts Press.

Swan-Miller, S. (2001). *An Empty Chair: Living in the Wake of a Sibling's Suicide.* Writer's Club Press.

Worden, J.W. (2002). *Children and Grief: When a Parent Dies.* Guilford Press.

Books for Teens

Crook, M. (2004). *Out of the Darkness: Teens Talk About Suicide*. Arsenal Pub Press.

Chalifour, F. (2005). *After*. Tundra Books.

Fitzgerald, H. (2000). *The Grieving Teen: A Guide for Teenagers and Their Friends*. Simon and Schuster.

Gootman, M. (2005). *When a Friend Dies: A Book for Teens About Grieving & Healing*. Free Spirit Publishing, Inc.

Horsley, H. & Horsley, G. (2007). *Teen Grief Relief: Parenting with Understanding, Supporting, and Guidance*. Rainbow Books.

Hughes, L.B. (2005). *You Are Not Alone: Teens Talk About Life After The Loss of a Parent*. Scholastic, Inc.

Myers, E. & Adams, K. (2006). *Teens, Loss, & Grief: The Ultimate Teen Guide*. Rowman & Littlefield Publishers, Inc.

Peacock, J. (2000). *Teen Suicide*. Capstone Press.

Perschy, M.K. (2004). *Helping Teens Work Through Grief* (2nd Edition). Brunner-Routledge.

Schab, L.M. (2008). *The Anxiety Workbook for Teens: Activities to Help You Deal with Anxiety & Worry*. Raincoast Books.

Sperekas, N. (2000). *SuicideWise: Taking Steps Against Teen Suicide*. Enslow.

Books for Parents and Professionals

Aldrich, L.M. (2001). *Facilitating Grief, Loss, and Trauma Support Groups: A Guidebook for Mental Health Professionals Dealing with Grief, Loss, and Trauma Issues Among Children and Adolescents.* M & K Publishing Co., Inc.

Aldrich, L.M. (2001). *Coping with Death in Our Schools: A Guidebook for School Personnel Dealing with the Death of a Student or Staff Member.* M & K Publishing Co., Inc.

Allen, J.G. (2005). *Coping with Trauma: Hope Through Understanding.* American Psychiatric Press.

Baugher, B. & Jordan, J. (2002). *After Suicide Loss: Coping with Your Grief.* Chevron Publishing.

Bolton, I. (2005). *My Son My Son: A Guide to Healing After Death, Loss, or Suicide.* MP3 Una Edition. Bolton Press.

Bowen, F. (2008). *Why: Spousal Survivor of Suicide.* XLibris Corporation.

Bryant, C. (2003). *Handbook of Death & Dying.* Sage Publications.

Carlson, T. (2000). *Suicide Survivors' Handbook.* Benline Press.

Cobain, B. & Larch, J. (2006). *Dying to Be Free: A Healing Guide for Families after a Suicide.* Hazelton.

Collins, J. (2003). *Sanity and Grace: A Journey of Suicide, Survival and Strength.* Putnam Pub Group.

Cox, A., David, C., & Arrington, C. (2003). *Aftershock: Help, Hope, and Healing in the Wake of Suicide.* Broadman and Holman Publishers.

Cox, P. (2002). *When Suicide Comes Home: A Father's Diary and Comments.* Bolten Press.

Deleon, C. (2004). *Dawning of a New Day: A Journey out of Darkness.* Inkwater Press.

Deverell, D. (2000). *Light Beyond the Darkness.* Clairview Books.

Di Ciacco, J.A. (2008). *The Colors of Grief: Understanding a Child's Journey Through Loss from Birth to Adulthood.* Jessica Kinglsey Publishers.

Doka, K. (2000). *Living with Grief: Children, Adolescents, and Loss.* Psychology Press.

Dyregrow, A. (2008). *Grief in Children: A Handbook for Adults.* Jessica Kingsley Publishers.

Dyregrov, A. (2008). *Grief in Young Children: A Handbook for Adults.* Jessica Kingsley Publishers.

Follette, V.M. & Ruzek, J.I. (2006). *Cognitive-Behavioral Therapies for Trauma* (2nd Ed.). Guilford Press.

Goldman, L. (2005). *Raising Our Children to Be Resilient: A Guide to Helping Children Cope with Trauma in Today's World.* Brunner-Routledge.

Goldman, L. (2001). *Breaking the Silence: A Guide to Help Children with Complicated Grief, Suicide, Homicide, AIDS, Violence, and Abuse.* Taylor & Francis.

Greenwald, R. (2005). *Child Trauma Handbook: A Guide for Helping Trauma-Exposed Children and Adolescents.* The Haworth Maltreatment and Trauma Press.

Harris Lord, J. (2006). *No Time for Goodbyes: Coping with Sorrow, Anger and Injustice After a Tragic Death.* (6th Ed.). Compassion Press.

Hart, P. (2001). *Survivors of Suicide.* New Page Books.

Hays, H. (2005). *Surviving Suicide: Help to Heal Your Heart.* Brown Books Publishing Group.

Hsu, A.Y. (2002). *Grieving a Suicide: A Loved One's Search for Comfort, Answers, and Hope.* InterVarsity Press.

Jackson, J. (2003). *SOS: A Handbook for Survivors of Suicide.* American Association of Suicidology.

Joiner, T. (2007). *Why People Die by Suicide.* Harvard University Press.

Kuehn, E. (2000). *After Suicide: Living with the Questions.* Capstone Press.

Kumar, S.M. (2005). *Grieving Mindfully: A Compassionate and Spiritual Guide to Coping With Loss.* New Harbinger Publications, Inc.

Leblanc, G. (2003). *Grieving the Unexpected: The Suicide of a Son.* Essence Publishing.

Leeuwenburgh, E. & Goldring, E. (2008). *Why Did You Die: Activities to Help Children Cope with Grief and Loss.* Instant Help Books.

Lester, D. (2003). *Katie's Diary: Unlocking the Mystery of Suicide.* Brunner-Routledge.

Linn-Gust, M. (2003). *Do They Have Bad Days in Heaven?* Bolten Press.

Lucas, C. & Seiden, H.M. (2007). *Silent Grief: Living in the Wake of Suicide.* Jessica Kingsley Publishers.

Markell, K.A. & Markell, M.A. (2008). *The Children Who Lived: Using Harry Potter and Other Fictional Characters to Help Grieving Children and Adolescents.* Routledge.

McCraken, A. & Semel, M. (2000). *A Broken Heart Still Beats After Your Child Dies.* Hazelden.

Mueller Bryson, K. (2006). *Those They Left Behind: Interviews, Stories, Essays and Poems by Survivors of Suicide.* Lulu.com.

Myers, M.F. & Fine C. (2006). *Touched by Suicide: Hope and Healing After Loss.* Gotham Books.

Noel, B. & Blair, P.B. (2008). *I Wasn't Ready to Say Goodbye: Surviving, Coping and Healing After the Sudden Death of a Loved One.* Sourcebooks, Inc.

O'Hara, K. & Gottlieb, D. (2006). *A Grief Like No Other: Surviving the Violent Death of Someone You Love.* Marlowe & Company.

Poussaint, A. & Alexander, A. (2000). *Lay My Burden Down: Unraveling Suicide and the Mental Health Crisis Among African-Americans.* Beacon Press.

Redfern, S. & Gilbert, S.K. (2008). *The Grieving Garden: Living with the Death of a Child.* Hampton Roads Publishing Company.

Requarth, M. (2006). *After a Parent's Suicide: Helping Children Heal.* Healing Hearts Press.

Reynolds, M. (2007). *Surviving Bill.* iUniverse.

Robinson, R. & Hart, P. (2001). *Survivors of Suicide.* Career Press.

Rothbaum, B.O., Foa, E.B., & Hembree, E.A. (2007). *Reclaiming Your Life from a Traumatic Experience: A Prolonged Exposure Treatment Program Workbook.* Oxford University Press.

Rubel, B. (2004). *Death, Dying, and Bereavement: Providing Compassion During a Time of Need.* Western Schools.

Rynerson, E.K. (2006). *Violent Death: Resilience and Intervention Beyond the Crisis.* University of Washington.

Smith, H.I. (2007). *Long-Shadowed Grief: Suicide and Its Aftermath.* Cowley Publications.

Smith, H.I. (2004). *When a Child You Love Is Grieving.* Beacon Hill Press of Kansas City.

Sorensen, J. (2008). *Overcoming Loss: Activities and Stories to Help Transform Children's Grief and Loss.* Jessica Kingsley Publishers.

Stark Hugus, C. (2008). *Crossing 13: Memoir of a Father's Suicide.* Affirm Publications.

Steel, D. (2000). *His Bright Light (The Story of Nick Traina).* Delta.

Stillwell, E.E. (2004). *The Death of a Child: Reflections for Grieving Parents.* ACTA Publications.

Swan-Miller, S. & Miller, M.B. (2000). *Empty Chair: Living in the Wake of a Sibling's Suicide.* Writers Club Press.

Underwood, S. (2004). *Eric's Story: Surviving a Son's Suicide.* Xlibris Publishing.

Wakenshaw, M. (2002). *Caring for Your Grieving Child: Engaging Activities for Dealing with Loss and Transition.* New Harbinger Publications.

Wertheimer A. (2001). *A Special Scar, The Experiences of People Bereaved by Suicide.* Psychology Press.

Wickershamm, J. (2008). *Suicide Index: Putting My Father's Life in Order.* Harcourt.

Williams, M.B. & Poijula, S. (2002). *PTSD Workbook: Simple, Effective Techniques for Overcoming Traumatic Stress Symptoms.* New Harbinger Publications.

Wilson, D. (2007). *From Suicide to Serenity: One Survivor's Story.* Booklocker.com.

Woelfel, J. (2002). *Meditations for Survivors of Suicide.* Catholic Book Publishing Company.

Wolfelt, A.D. (2004). *A Child's View of Grief: A Guide for Parents, Teachers, and Counselors.* Companion Press.

Woolley, B. (2006). *If Only: Personal Stories of Loss Through Suicide.* UWA Press.

Wroebleski, A. (2002). *Suicide Survivors: A Guide for Those Left Behind.* Afterwords Pub.

Zastrow, N. (2007). *Ask Me: 30 Things I Want You to Know About Being a Survivor of Suicide.* Centering Corporation.

Ziontz Fox, J. & Roldan, M. (2009). *Voices of Strength: Sons and Daughters of Suicide Speak Out.* New Horizons Press.

Resources and Support

Alive Alone
www.alivealone.org

American Academy of Child and Adolescent Psychiatry
(AACAP)
www.aacap.org

American Association of Suicidology (AAS)
202-237-2280
www.suicidology.org

American Foundation for Suicide Prevention (AFSP)
1-888-333-2377
www.afsp.org

American Hospice Foundation
202-223-0204
www.americanhospice.org

Association for Death Education and Counseling (ADEC)
860-586-7503
www.adec.org

Bereaved Parents of the U.S.A.
708-748-7866
www.bereavedparentsusa.org

Bereavement Publishing, Inc.
888-604-4673
www.bereavementmag.com

Centering Corporation and Grief Digest Magazine
Education and Resources for the Bereaved
402-553-1200
www.centering.org

Centre for Suicide Prevention (SIEC)
Calgary, AB, T2G 5A5
403-245-3900
www.suicideinfo.ca/

Chabereth (Christian) Ministries, Inc.
Healing Hearts Ministries; Ministry to Suicide Survivors
302-478-2575
www.mysite.verizon.net/chabereth/healing_hearts.html

The Child Trauma Academy
www.childtrauma.org

Compassion Books
Exceptional resources to help people through loss and grief
828-675-5909
www.compassionbooks.com

Compassionate Friends
630-990-0246, 877-969-0010
www.compassionatefriends.com

Fatal Mistakes: Families Shattered by Suicide DVD
This 45-minute Emmy Award-winning documentary features
Barbara Rubel and several families coping with suicide.
They share their common experience with the hope they will
comfort others experiencing similar grief. Video includes
interviews with leading researchers and clinicians, including
Jan Fawcett, M.D., Frederick K. Goodwin, M.D., David
Schafer, M.D., David Clark, Ph.D., J. John Mann, M.D.,

Kay Redfield Jamison, Ph.D., and Alec Roy, M.D.
DVD produced by the American Foundation for Suicide
Prevention and hosted by Emmy Award-winning Best Actress,
Mariette Hartley. To order DVD: Web: www.afsp.org
888-333-AFSP

Friends For Survival, Inc.
A national outreach program for survivors of suicide
916-392-0664
www.friendsforsurvival.org

Friends and Family of Suicide
www.pos-ffos.com

Friends and Families of Suicides Memorial Website
www.friendsandfamiliesofsuicide.com

Gift of Keith
www.thegiftofkeith.org

Good Grief Resources
www.goodgriefresources.com

Good Grief Rituals
www.goodgriefrituals.com

Grief Digest Quarterly Magazine
A Centering Corporation Resource
1-866-218-0101
www.griefdigest.com

Grief Healing
www.griefhealing.com

GriefNet.org
www.griefnet.org.

Griefwork Center, Inc.
Providing professional keynote speaker services on Coping
with Suicide and Traumatic Loss, and Building Professional
Resiliency: Preventing Burnout and Compassion Fatigue
732-422-0400
www.griefworkcenter.com

Heartbeat
719-596-2575
www.heartbeatsurvivorsaftersuicide.org/index.shtml

Hospice Foundation of America
202-638-5419
1-800-854-3402
www.hospicefoundation.org

In-Sight Books: Training and Resources
(800) 658-9262
www.insightbooks.com

The Jason Foundation
www.jasonfoundation.com

Kristen Books Hope Center & The National Hopeline
Network
703-837-3364
www.hopeline.com

LegacyConnect
Discussions and Group Forums
www.connect.legacy.com

Lifekeeper Foundation
678-937-9297
www.lifekeeper.org

Loving Outreach
www.lovingoutreach.org/index.html

National Center for Death Education; Mount Ida College
www.mountida.edu/sp.cfm?pageid=307

National Center for Suicide Prevention Training (NCSPT)
www.ncsp.org

National Funeral Director's Association Consumer
Resources
www.nfda.org

National Organization for People of Color Against Suicide
866-899-5317
www.nopcas.com

Parents of Suicide
www.pos-ffos.com

The Samaritans
www.befrienders.org

Sharing and Healing
www.sharingandhealing.org

SiblingsSurvivors.com
www.siblingsurvivors.com

Suicide Awareness/Voices of Education (SAVE)
952-946-7998
www.save.org

Suicide Discussion Board
www.suicidediscussionboard.com/

Share Grief
www.sharegrief.com

The Suicide Memorial Wall
www.suicidememorialwall.com.

Suicide Prevention Action Network USA (SPAN USA)
SPAN has merged with www.AFSP.org
www.spanusa.org

Suicide Prevention News and Comment (SPNAC)
Lifeline Gallery
www.suicidepreventioncommunity.wordpress.com/category/
grief/

Suicide Prevention Resource Center (SPRC)
www.sprc.org

Suicide Wall Homepage
www.suicidewall.com

Surviving Suicide
www.survivingsuicide.com

Survivors Of Law Enforcement Suicide (SOLES)
www.tearsofacop.com

The Survivors of Loved Ones' Suicide (SOLOS)
www.1000deaths.com

Survivors of Suicide
www.survivorsofsuicide.com

Survivors of Suicide, Inc. (SOS)
www.sossd.org

Tragedy Assistance Programs for Survivors (TAPS)
Providing comfort 24 hours a day to those grieving the
sudden death of a loved one in the military.
800-959-8277
www.taps.org.

Read Barbara Rubel's article online. Rubel, B. (2008)
Suicide in the Military, *TAPS Quarterly Magazine,
Vol. 14*(2). 28-29.
www.taps.org/uploadedFiles/TAPS/RESOURCES/
Magazines/Magazine-Summer08.pdf

Web Healing
Teaching interactive articles and contacts
www.webhealing.com

With One Voice
www.withonevoice.com

Yellow Ribbon Suicide Prevention Program
303-429-3530
www.yellowribbon.org

Adult Bereavement Support Groups After a Suicide

Many bereaved individuals after a suicide find help through support groups. These support groups offer an opportunity to share grief with others who have experienced a similar loss. The American Foundation for Suicide Prevention (AFSP) support group directory is organized by state. AFSP makes their directory available as a public service and do not recommend or endorse any of the particular groups listed.

www.afsp.org
Click: Surviving Suicide Loss
Scroll down to: Support Groups
Scroll down to: To Find a Support Group Click Here
Select a state and view the support groups listed

Grief Programs Serving Children, Teens, and Families Across the United States

Listed by State

The Amelia Center
Birmingham, AL 35233
205-251-3430
www.ameliacenter.org

The Caring House
Huntsville, AL 35805
888-619-8000
www.hospicefamilycare.org

Healing House Community Bereavement Center
Decatur, AL 35601
256-584-0058
www.hospiceofthevalley.net

The Healing Place: A Center for Loss & Change, Inc.
Tuscumbia, AL 35674
256-383-7133
www.thehealthplaceinfo.org

Hospice Family Care
Huntsville, AL 35805
256-650-1212

Hospice of Cullman County
Cullman, AL 35055
256-739-5185

Hospice of EAMC
Auburn, AL 36830
334-826-1899

Hospice of Marshall Co., Inc.
Albertville, AL 35950
888-334-9336
www.hospicemc.org

Wiregrass Hospice Inc.
Dothan, AL 36303
800-626-1101
www.wiregrasshospice.org

Forget Me Not Grief Program
Anchorage, AK 99518
907-561-5322
www.hospiceofanchorage.org

Arkansas Children's Hospital: Center for
Good Mourning
Little Rock, AR 72202
501-364-7000
www.archildrens.org/community_outreach/cent

Kaleidoscope Kids
Little Rock, AR 72207
877-357-5437
www.kaleidoscopekids.org

Children To Children
Tucson, AZ 85719-1313
520-322-9155
www.tunidito.org

Grief Speak: Hospice of the Valley
Phoenix, AZ 85014
602-530-6987
www.hospiceofthevalley.org

New Song Center for Grieving Children
Scottsdale, AZ 85253
480-951-8985
www.thenewsongcenter.org

Safe Harbor Support, Inc.
Gilbert, AZ 85299
480-214-5728
www.safe-harborsupportinc.org

Stepping Stones of Hope, Inc.
Phoenix, AZ 85014
602-264-7520
www.steppingstonesofhope.org

Tu Nidito Children & Family Services
Tucson, AZ 85719
520-322-9155
www.tunidito.org

After School Counseling Services
Burlingame, CA 94010
650-558-1015

Art & Creativity for Healing
Laguna Niguel, CA 92677
949-367-1902
www.art4healing.org

Camarillo Hospice
Camarillo, CA 93010
805-389-6870
www.camarillohospice.org

Camp Good Grief - Loma/Linda University
Loma Linda, CA 92354
909-558-4073
www.llu.edu

Camp Hope
Livermore, CA 94550
619-594-4389
www.camphopeca.com

Center for Grief Care and Education: San Diego Hospice
San Diego, CA 92103
619-278-6480

The Center for Grief and Loss
Los Angeles, CA 90044
213-924-3510
www.griefcenterforchildren.org

The Center for Grief and Loss
Pasadena, CA 91106 and Glendale, CA 91202
866-74GRIEF
www.griefcenterforchildren.org

Centre for Living with Dying
Santa Clara, CA 95050
408-553-6950
www.thecentre.org

CHANGES: Grief Support for Grieving Children & Families
Pathways Hospice
Long Beach, CA 90805
562-531-3031
www.pathwayshospice.org

Children's Bereavement Art Group
Sacramento, CA 95816
916-454-6555
www.sutterchildrens.org/childbereavement

Circle of Care
Oakland, CA 94602
510-531-7551
www.ebac.org/programs

Comfort for Kids
Concord, CA 94520
925-609-1830
www.hospicecc.org

Common Threads At Inland Hospice
Claremont, CA 91711
909-399-3289
www.inlandhospice.org

Community Hospice, Inc.
Modesto, CA 95350
209-577-0615
www.hospiceheart.org

Contra Costa Crisis Center
Walnut Creek, CA 94598
925-944-0645 24 hour toll-free
www.crisis-center.org

Drew's Place
Nevada City, CA 95959
530-265-0341

Didi Hirsch Community Mental Health Center
Culver City, CA 90230
310-390-6612
www.didihirsch.org

Elizabeth Hospice
Escondido, CA 92025
760-737-2050
www.elizabethhospice.org

Footsteps of Saint Agnes
Fresno, CA 93720
559-450-5608
www.samc.com

Gary A. Garcia Foundation
Los Angeles, CA 90026
213-482-8500
www.garyagarcia.org

Gary's Place for Kids
Laguna Hills, CA 92653
949-461-9780
www.garysplaceforkids.org

The Gathering Place
Redondo Beach, CA 90277
310-374-6323
www.griefcenter.info

Good Grief for Kids: Community Hospital of the Monterey
Penin
Monterey, CA 93942
831-625-4753
www.chomp.org

Greater Hope Foundation
Barstow, CA 92311
760-256-0432
www.homepage.mac.com/gdandscompserv/home01.htm

Grief Recovery Institute
Sherman Oaks, CA 91413
818-907-9600
www.grief.net

Griefbusters: Hospice of the Central Coast
Salinas, CA 93901
831-658-3772
www.chomp.org

Griefbusters of Amador
Jackson, CA 95665
209-223-5500

The Healing Center for Grieving Children
Folsom, CA 95630
916-791-8414
www.grievingchild.net

Heartland Home, Health Care & Hospice
Riverside, CA 92507
951-369-8640
www.hcrmanorcaren.com

Hinds Hospice Center for Grief and Loss
Fresno, CA 93711
559-248-8579
www.hindshospice.org

Hope Bereavement Center
Carlsbad, CA 92008
760-431-4100
www.hospicenorthcoast.org

Hope Hospice: Children's & Family Grief Services
Dublin, CA 94568
925-829-8770
www.hopehospice.com

Hospice of Hunboldt Bereavement Services
Eureka, CA 95501
707-445-8445

Hospice of Marin - Youth Bereavement Program
Larkspur, CA 94939
415-526-5549
www.hospiceofmarin.org

Hospice of Petaluma Children and Teen Program
Petaluma, CA 94952
707-778-6242

Hospice of the North Coast Community Outreach
Carlsbad, CA 92008
760-431-4100
www.hospicenorthcoast.org

H.U.G. (Health Understanding of Grief) of Hospice
Caring Project
Scotts Valley, CA 95066
831-430-3000

Josie's Place for Bereaved Youth and Families
San Francisco, CA 94110
415-513-6343
www.josiesplace.org

KARA Grief Support
Palo Alto, CA 94301
650-321-5272
www.kara-grief.org

Mourning Star Center of the VNAIC—Palm Desert
Palm Desert, CA 92211
760-836-0360
www.mourningstar.org

Mourning Star Center of the VNAIC—Victorville
Victorville, CA 92345
760-241-3564 x250
www.mourningstar.org

New Hope Grief Support Community
Long Beach, CA 90808
562-429-0075
www.newhopegrief.org

Our House: A Grief Support Center
Los Angeles, CA 90025
310-475-0299
www.ourhouse-grief.org

Our House: A Grief Support Center
Woodland Hills, CA 91364
818-222-3344
www.ourhouse-grief.org

Parents Helping Parents
Sonora, CA 95370
209-768-9139

Sutter VNA & Hospice Child/Teen Bereavement Program
Santa Rosa, CA 95401
707-535-5700
www.suttervnahospice.org

Touchstone Support Network
Santa Clara, CA 95054-3222
408-727-5775
www.php.com

Willmar Center for Bereaved Children
Sonoma, CA 95476
707-935-1946

Wings of Hope Hospice Services of Lake County
Lakeport, CA 95453
707-263-6222
www.hospice-lakecountyca.org

Yolo Hospice
Davis, CA 95617
800-491-7711 toll-free
www.yolohospice.org

Healing Circles: HospiceCare Grief and Education Center
Boulder, CO 80303
303-604-5330
www.hospicecareonline.org

Hospice and Palliative Care of Western Colorado
Child and Teen Center
Grand Junction, CO 81506
970-263-2193
www.gvhospice.com

Hospice of Metro Denver: The Footprints Grief Center
Denver, CO 80246-1234
303-321-2828
www.hmd.org

Judi's House: The Judith Ann Griese Foundation
Denver, CO 80206
720-941-0331
www.judithouse.org

The Center for Hope, Inc.
Darien, CT 06820
203-655-4693
www.centerforhope.org

The Cove Center for Grieving Children
Meriden, CT 06450
800-750-COVE
www.covect.org

The Cove/West Hartford
West Hartford, CT 06119
203-494-3712

The Den For Grieving Kids/Family Centers, Inc.
Greenwich, CT 06830
203-869-4848
www.familycenters.org\children.html

The Healing Hearts Center for Grieving Children & Families
Danbury, CT 06810-4710
203-797-1685
www.regionalhospicect.org/healing_hearts

Mary's Place: A Center for Grieving Children & Families
Windsor, CT 06095
860-688-9621
www.marysplacect.com

Delaware Hospice
Georgetown, DE 19947
800-838-9800 toll-free
www.delawarehospice.org

Supporting Kidds: The Center for Grieving Children
Hockessin, DE 19707
302-235-5544
www.supportingkidds.org

Wendt Center for Loss and Healing
NW, Washington, DC 20008
202-624-0010
www.wendtcenter.org

Begin Again Children's Grief Center
Daytona Beach, FL 32114
386-258-5100

Bright Star Center for Grieving Children
West Melbourne, FL 32904
321-733-7672

Caring Tree Program of Big Bend Hospice, Inc.
Tallahassee, FL 32308
850-878-5310 or 800-772-5862
www.bigbendhospice.org

Catholic Hospice
Miami Lakes, FL 33014
305-822-2380
www.catholichospice.org

Children's Bereavement Center
South Miami, FL 3314
305-668-4902
www.childbereavement.org

Circle of Love Center for Grieving Children
LifePath Hospice & Palliative Care, Inc.
Tampa, FL 33609
800-209-2200
www./lifepath-hospice.org/patients/center.html

Community Hospice of NE Florida: Grief and Loss Center
Jacksonville, FL 33257
904-268-5200

Hearts and Hope, Inc.
West Palm Beach, FL 33401
561-832-1913
www.heartsandhope.org

Hope Hospice Rainbow Center
Fort Myers, FL 33908
800-835-1673
www.hopehospice.org

Horizons Bereavement Center: Hospice of Palm Beach
County
West Palm Beach, FL 33407
561-848-5200 (hospice)
www.hpbc.com

Horizons Children's Loss Program
Altamonte Springs, FL 32714
407-682-0808

Hospice by the Sea, Inc.
Boca Raton, FL 33486-3395
561-395-5031
www.hospicebytheseafl.org

Hospice of Citrus Cty - Wings Grief Support Teams
Beverly Hills, FL 34464
352-527-2020
www.hospiceofcitruscounty.org

Hospice of Lake & Sumter, Inc.
Tavares, FL 32778
352-742-6888

Hospice of St. Francis: North Star Program
Titusville, FL 32780
321-269-4240
www.hospiceofstfrancis.com

Hospice of the Emerald Coast
Panama City, FL 32405
877-717-7357 toll-free
www.hospiceemeraldcoast.org

Kathy's Place: A Center for Grieving Children
Tampa, FL 33609
813-541-2672
www.aplace4hope.org

Lee's Place
Tallahassee, FL 32303
850-841-7733
www.leesplace.org

Mending Hearts Children's Program: Gulfside Regional
Hospice
New Port Richey, FL 34652
727-844-3946

New Hope for Kids
Maitland, FL 32751
407-599-0909
www.newhopeforkids.org

North Star
Titusville, FL 32780
321-264-1687
www.hospiceofstfrancis.com

The Bright Star Center for Grieving Children: Hospice of
Health First
Melbourne, FL 32901
321-733-7672

Tomorrow's Rainbow
Coconut Creek, FL 33073
954-978-2390
www.tomorrowsrainbow.org

Camp Magik
Dunwoody, GA 30338
770-396-7995 Ext. 13
www.CampMagik.org

Full Circle Grief & Loss Center: Hospice of Savannah
Savannah, GA 31406
888-355-4911 toll-free
www.hospicesavannah.org

Hope for Grieving Children
Roswell, GA 30075
770-915-2537
www.rfbc.org

Kate's Club
Atlanta, GA 30355
770-618-4474
www.katesclub.org

National Resource Center for Suicide Prevention and
Aftercare:
The Link Counseling Center
Atlanta, GA 30328
404-256-9797
www.thelink.org

Odyssey Family Counseling Center
Hapeville, GA 30354
404-669-3462
www.odysseycounseling.org

Rising Sun Center for Loss and Renewal
Marietta, GA 30066
770-928-1027
www.risingsuncenter.com

Hospice Hawaii
Honolulu, HI 96817-5018
808-924-9255
www.hospicehawaii.org

Kauai Hospice: Forget Me Not
Lihue, HI 96766
808-245-7277

Kids Hurt Too
Honolulu, HI 96828
808-735-2989
www.grievingyouth.org

Outreach for Grieving Youth Alliance (OGYA)
Honolulu, HI 96828
808-735-2989
www.grievingyouth.org

Bonner Community Hospice
Sandpoint, ID 83864
208-265-1185

Hospice of North Idaho
Hayden, ID 83835
208-772-7994

Kids Count Too!
Twin Falls, ID 83301
800-540-4061 toll-free

The Touchstone Center for Grieving Children
Boise, ID 83712
208-377-3216
www.touchstonecenter.org

Willow Center
Lewiston, ID 83501
509-780-1156

Adventist St. Thomas Hospice "Tommy's Kids" & Tommy's
Kids Summer Camp
Bun Ridge, IL 60527
630-856-6993

Buddy's Place of Pillars
Western Springs, IL 60558
708-354-5280
www.pillarscommunity.org

Camp Courageous: Methodist Medical Center
Peoria, IL 61636-0002
309-672-5746

Center for Grief Recovery: Institute for Creativity
Chicago, IL 60626
773-274-4600
www.griefcounselor.bigstep.com

Fox Valley Hospice: Herbie's Friends/Grief Takes a Hike
Geneva, IL 60134
630-232-2233
www.foxvalleyhospice.net

Good Mourning Program at Rainbow Hospice
Park Ridge, IL 60068
847-685-9900
www.rainbowhospice.org

Heartlight: Children's Memorial Hospital
Chicago, IL 60614-3394
773-975-8829
www.childrensmemorial.org

Heartlinks: Children's Bereavement Program
Swansea, IL 62223
618-277-1800

Hospice of Northeastern Illinois Bereavement Program
Barrington, IL 60010
847-381-5599
www.hospiceanswers.org

Hospice Partners/Sunrise Program
Hillside, IL 60162
708-234-2800
www.hospicepartners.net

Kid's Time Grief Support Group: St. Elizabeth's Hospital
Belleville, IL 62222-1998
618-234-2120
www.steliz.org

Rainbows, Inc. International
Rolling Meadows, IL 60008-4231
800-266-3206
www.rainbows.org

Brooke's Place for Grieving Young People, Inc.
Indianapolis, IN 46240
317-705-9650
www.brookesplace.org

Erin's House for Grieving Children, Inc.
Fort Wayne, IN 46804
260-423-2466
www.erinshouse.org

Legacy House, Inc.
Indianapolis, IN 46218
317-554-5272
www.legacy-house.org

Living with Grief Support Group
Winamac, IN 46996
574-946-2100

Mending Hearts: Boys and Girls Clubs of Wayne County
Richmond, IN 47374
765-962-6922
www.bgcrichmond.org

Ryan's Place
Goshen, IN 46527
574-535-1000
www.ryans-place.org

The Center for Mental Health
Anderson, IN 46012
765-649-8161
www.cfmh.org

Amanda the Panda
Des Moines, IA 50311
515-223-HUGS
www.AmandaThePanda.org

Children's Grief Support
Pella, IA 50219
641-620-5050
www.pellahealth.org

Eucalyptus Tree Program: Cedar Valley Hospice
Waterloo, IA 50704-2880
800-617-1972 toll-free
www.cvhospice.org

Grief Support Services
Waterloo, IA 50704
517-272-2002
www.cvhospice.org

Iowa City Hospice
Iowa City, IA 52240
319-351-5665
www.iowacityhospice.org

Rick's House of Hope for Grieving & Traumatized Children
Davenport, IA 52803
563-324-9580
www.genesishealth.com

Solace House
Shawnee Mission, KS 66208
913-341-0318
www.solacehouse.org

The Guidance Center
Leavenworth, KS 66048
913-682-5118
www.theguidance-ctr.org/

Three Trees Center
Wichita, KS 67226
316-683-2081 toll-free
www.threetrees.org

RENEW Center for Personal Recovery
Berea, KY 40403
859-986-7878
www.renew.net

Seasons Grief Center
Metairie, LA 70005
504-834-5957
www.seasonsgriefcenter.org

The Healing House
Lafayette, LA 70502
337-234-0443
www.healing-house.org

Camp Ray of Hope
Waterville, ME 04901
207-873-3615

The Center for Grieving Children
Portland, ME 04101
207-775-5216
www.cgcmaine.org

BRIDGES Calvert Hospice Care and Resource Center
Prince Frederick, MD 20678
410-535-5677
www.calverthospice.org

Children's Friend
Worcester, MA 01609
508-753-5425
www.childrensfriend.org

Cranberry Hospice of CURA VNA
Plymouth, MA 02360
508-746-0215
www.bereavementservciesma.org

The Children's Room
Arlington and Framingham, MA
781-641-4741
www.childrensroom.org

The Garden: A Center for Grieving Children & Teens
Northampton, MA 01061
413-584-3796
www.garden-cgc.org

The Good Grief Program: Boston Medical Center
Boston, MA 02118
617-414-7915
www.thegoodgriefprogram.org

Braveheart Grief Services: Arbor Hospice and
Home Care
Ann Arbor, MI 48103
734-662-5999 x161
www.braveheartofmichigan.org

Ele's Place
Lansing, MI 48915
517-482-1315
www.elesplace.org

For the Kids Foundation
Birmingham, MI 48009-6306
888-987-5437
www.forthekidsfoundation.org

The National Institute for Trauma and Loss in Children
Grosse Pointe Woods, MI 48236
313-885-0390
www.tlcinstitute.org

Lory's Place: Hospice at Home Inc.
Saint Joseph, MI 49085
800-717-3812
www.lorysplace.org

New Hope Center for Grief Support: New Hope for KIDZ &
TEENS
Northville, MI 48167
248-348-0115
www.newhopecenter.net

Katlin's Gift
Rochester, MN 55901
507-282-7932
www.katlinsgift.org

St. Mary's Grief Support Center: St. Mary's Medical Center
Duluth, MN 55805
218-786-4402
www.stmarysduluth.otherservices.org
(Click: Go to Other Services)

The Minnesota Foundation for Children
Plymouth, MN 55441
763-550-0157
www.campamandaminn.com

McClean Fletcher Center
Jackson, MS 39216
601-982-4406
www.jljackson.org/?nd=20052026

Annie's Hope: The Bereavement Center for Kids
St. Louis, MO 63122
314-965-5015
www.annieshope.org

KAPstone House Inc.
Joplin, MO 64801
417-781-8185
www.kapstonehouse.org/index.html

Lost and Found: A Place for Hope and Grief
Springfield, MO 65802
417-832-9423
www.lostandfoundozarks.com

Missouri Baptist Medical Center Grief Support Program
Saint Louis, MO 63131
314-997-5057
www.missouribaptistmedicalcenter.org

The Missouri Baptist Medical Center
Saint Louis, MO 63131
314-997-5057
www.missouribaptistmedicalcenter.org

River Stone Hospice: Brave Hearts
Billings, MT 59101
406-247-3300
www.riverstonehealth.org

Mourning Hope Grief Center
Lincoln, NE 68516
402-423-1416
www.mourninghope.org

Ted E. Bear Hollow
Omaha, NE 68104
402-502-2773
www.tedebearhollow.org

Camp Mariposa
Las Vegas, NV 89015
702-796-3159
www.nah.org

Solacetree, Inc.
Reno, NV 89505
775-324-7723
www.solacetree.org

Bridges for Children & Teens: Seacoast Hospice
Exeter, NH 03833
603-778-7391
www.seacoasthospice.org

Pete's Place
Dover, NH 03820
603-740-2689

The Alcove Center for Grieving Children & Families
Northfield, NJ 08225
609-484-1133
www.thealcove.org

Children's Art Therapy Program at Riverview
Red Bank, NJ 07701
732-530-2382
www.meridianhealth.com

Comfort Zone Camp North
North Caldwell, NJ 07006
201-420-0081
www.comfortzonecamp.org

Good Grief, Inc.
Summit, NJ 07901
908-251-5101
www.good-grief.org

JFK Medical Center
Haven Hospice
Edison, NJ 08818-3059
732-321-7769

The Wellness Community of Central New Jersey
Bedminster, NJ 07921
908-658-5400 ext 2
www.thewellnesscommunity.org

Wings of Hope Programs for Continuing Support Svcs.
Medford, NJ 08055
609-714-0868

Children's Grief Center of New Mexico, Inc.
Albuquerque, NM 87154
505-323-0478
www.childrensgrief.org

Gerard's House
Santa Fe, NM 87592
505-424-1800
www.gerardshouse.org

Center for Hope: Schneider Children's Hospital
New Hyde Park, NY 11040
718-470-3123

Center for Living with Loss Hospice & Palliative Care
Associates for NY
Liverpool, NY 13088-6168
315-634-1100
www.hospicecny.org

Haven Grief Counseling Center Grieving Children's Program
Schenectady, NY 12305
518-370-1666
www.havengriefcounselingcenter.org

Heartbridge
New York, NY 10025
212-865-6742
www.heartbridgecenter.org

Hope for the Bereaved, Inc.
Syracuse, NY 13219
315-475-4673
www.hopeforbereaved.com

Hospice Care Network
Westbury, NY 11590
516-832-7100
www.hospicecarenetwork.org

Jewish Board of Family & Children Services: Loss &
Bereavement Program
New York, NY 10019
212-632-4692
www.jbfcs.org

Metropolitan Hospice of Greater NY
Brooklyn, NY 11220-4711
718-921-7900
www.metropolitanhospice.org

New Insights, Inc.
Middle Grove, NY 12866
518-893-2012

South Nassau Communities Hospital Counseling Center
Baldwin, NY 11510
516-546-1370

St. Mary's Hospital for Children Pastoral Care Department
Bayside, NY 11360
718-281-8852
www.stmaryskids.org

Storm Clouds & Rainbows Life Transitions Center
Buffalo, NY 14215-2045
716-836-6460
www.palliativecare.org

The Bereavement Center, Hospice, Inc.
Poughkeepsie, NY 12601
800-522-9132
www.hospiceinc.org

The Bereavement Center for Support & Healing
Brooklyn, NY 11201
718-722-6214
www.ccbq.org/bereavement.htm

The Caring Circle: Westchester School for Special Children
Yonkers, NY 10701
914-666-4228
www.hospiceofwestchester.com

The Caring Circle Hospice Care in Westchester and Putnam
Mount Kisco, NY 10549
914-666-4228
www.hospiceofwestchester.com

The Children's Grieving Center Hospice
Newburgh, NY 12550
800-924-0157
www.hospiceoforange.com

The Healing Center: Long Island College Hospital
Brooklyn, NY 11201
718-780-2942
www.healingcenterkids.org

The Roberts Wahls Bereavement Center Hospice, Inc.
Kingston, NY 12401
800-522-9132
www.hospiceinc.org

The Sanctuary
Larchmont, NY 10538-1448
914-834-4906
www.thesanctuaryforgrief.org

The Schnurmacher Family Bereavement and
Trauma Center
Roslyn Heights, NY 11577
516-626-1971

The Tree House Program
Tuckahoe, NY 10707
914-961-2818
www.treehouse-bcw.org or www.thebereavementcenter.org

Visiting Nurse Hospice Care Bereavement Program
New York, NY 10001-3797
212-609-1979
www.vnsny.org/mainsite/services/s_hospice.html

Payne Whitney Childhood Bereavement Program, NY
888-694-5700
www.wo-pub2.med.cornell.edu/cgi-bin/WebObjects/
PublicA.woa/wa/viewService?servicesID=1463&website=
wmc+psych

Wounded Healers Bereavement Support Group, Inc.
Auburn, NY 13021
315-252-5166
www.woundedhealers.com

Busch Family Funeral Chapels Bereavement Care
Cleveland, OH 44109
800-252-8724, 216-741-7700
www.buschfuneral.com

Camp Courageous
Troy, OH 45373
937-335-5191

Cornerstone of Hope
Independence, OH 44131
216-524-3787
www.cornerstoneofhope.org

Fernside: A Center for Grieving Children
Cincinnati, OH 45242-5644
513-745-0111
www.fernside.org

Joel's Place for Children
Moreland Hills, OH 44022
440-248-4412
www.joelsplaceforchildren.com

Mount Carmel Hospice Evergreen Center
Columbus, OH 43215
614-234-0200
www.hchs.org

Oak Tree Corner, Inc.
Dayton, OH 45419-1512
937-285-0199
www.oaktreecorner.com

Willow Wood
Amelia, OH 45147
513-753-6464
www.willowwood.org

A Place of Hope
Bartlesville, OK 74006
918-336-1510
www.geocities.com/aplaceofhope

Calm Waters Center for Children and Families
Oklahoma City, OK 73116
405-841-4800
www.calmwaters.org

Kaleidoscope
Norman, OK 73072
405-306-0052

The Kid's Place
Edmond, OK 73083
405-844-5437
www.kidsplace.org

The Tristesse Grief Center Inc.
Tulsa, OK 74119
918-587-1200
www.thetristessecenter.org

Courageous Kids: Hospice of Sacred Heart
Eugene, OR 97402
541-461-7577
www.peacehealth.org

The Dougy Center for Grieving Children
Portland, OR 97286
503-775-5683
www.dougy.org

Hope House: Lutheran Community Services
Astoria, OR 97103
503-325-6754

Light House Center
Coos Bay, OR 97420
541-269-2986

Mercy Medical Center Hospice: Wings of Hope
Roseburg, OR 97470
541-677-2384

Mother Oak's Child Center for Grieving Children:
Willamette Valley Hospice
Salem, OR 97304
800-555-2431
www.wvh.org

Winterspring
Medford, OR 97501
541-772-2527
www.winterspring.org

Caring Place
Pittsburgh, PA 15222
888-224-4673
www.wpacaringfoundation.com

The Center for Loss and Bereavement: Nello's Corner
Skippack, PA 19474
610-222-4110
www.bereavementcenter.org/nello.htm

The Center for Traumatic Stress in Children and
Adolescents:
Allegheny General Hospital, Dept. of Psychiatry
Pittsburgh, PA 15212
412-330-4328
www.pittsburghchildtrauma.com

Center for Grieving Children, Teens & Families
Philadelphia, PA 19134-1095
215-427-6767
www.grievingchildren.org

Children's Hospital of Philadelphia Bereavement Program
Philadelphia, PA 19104-4399
215-590-3273
www.chop.edu

Daddy's Spirit Moves Me Forward
Valley Forge, PA 19484
610-710-1477
www.DaddysSpirit.org

Highmark Caring Place
Pittsburg, PA 15222
888-224-4673
www.highmarkcaringplace.com

Highmark Caring Place
Erie, PA 16507
866-212-4673
www.highmarkcaringplace.com

Highmark Caring Place
Lemoyne, PA 17043
866-613-4673
www.highmarkcaringplace.com

Hospice Care, Inc.
Waynesburg, PA 15370-8084
724-228-4580
www.welnet.org

Mommy's Light Lives On
Lionville, PA 19353
610-725-9790
www.mommyslight.org

Peter's Place: A Center for Grieving Children & Families
Berwyn, PA 19312
610-889-7400

Safe Harbor Program: Abington Memorial Health Center
Willow Grove, PA 19090
215-481-5983
www.amh.org/healthsrv/wcsafhar.htm

Friends Way
Warwick, RI 02889
401-921-0980
www.friendsway.org

Good Grieving: Helping Children and Teens: South Carolina
Cancer Center
Columbia, SC 29203
803-434-3500
www.sccancercenter.org

The Grief Center: Alive Hospice, Inc.
Nashville, TN 37203
615-963-4662
www.alivehospice.org

Bo's Place
Houston, TX 77054
713-942-8339
www.bosplace.org

Building Bridges Hospice of San Angelo
San Angelo, TX 76902
325-658-6524
www.hospiceofsanangelo.org

Camp El Tesoro de la Vida: First Texas Council of
Camp Fire
Fort Worth, TX 76137-4699
817-831-2111
www.firsttexascampfire.org

Camp Sol, Inc.
Dallas, TX 75204
214-442-1664
www.campsol.org

Children's Grief Center of El Paso
El Paso, TX 79901
915-532-6004
www.cgcelpaso.org

Dallas Kids GriefWorks, Christian Services
Dallas, TX 75240
972-960-9981
www.christian-works.org

Elijah's Place: Catholic Charities
Beaumont, TX 77704
409-835-7118
www.catholiccharitiesbmt.org

Gili's Place for the Bereaved
Houston, TX 77225
713-661-9209
www.gilisplace.com

Hope Hospice Children's Grief Program
New Braunfels, TX 78130
800-499-7501
www.hopehospice.net

Hospice Austin: Camp Brave Heart
Austin, TX 78759
512-342-4700
www.hospiceaustin.org

Journey of Hope Grief Support Center, Inc. serving the
Dallas Metroplex
Plano, TX 75075
972-964-1600
www.johgriefsupport.org

Project Joy and Hope for Texas
Pasadena, TX 77508
713-944-6JOY, 866-JOY HOPE
www.joyandhope.org

The Children's Bereavement Center of South Texas
San Antonio, TX 78212
210-736-HUGS (4847)
www.cbcst.org

The Hope & Healing Place
Amarillo, TX 79102
806-371-8998
www.hopeandhealingplace.org

The Warm Place
Fort Worth, TX 76104-2710
817-870-2272
www.thewarmplace.org

Wings Children's Grief Program: Hospice of East Texas
Tyler, TX 75701
903-266-3400
www.hospice-etex.com

Wings Program: Houston Hospice
Houston, TX 77024
281-587-2218
www.houstonhospice.org

The Family Summit Foundation: A Center for Grieving
Children
South Ogden, UT 84403
801-476-1127
www.familysummit.com

The Sharing Place
Salt Lake City, UT 84106
801-466-6730
www.thesharingplace.com

Camp Comfort Zone
Richmond, VA 23230
866-488-5679
www.ComfortZoneCamp.org

Jewish Family Service of Tidewater, Inc.
Virginia Beach, VA 23462
757-459-4640
www.jfshamptonroads.org

Kids' Haven: A Center for Grieving Children
Lynchburg, VA 24503
434-845-4072

Center For Counseling and Development: Safe Harbor
Olympia, WA 98501-1522
360-754-0820

Children Grieve Too
Renton, WA 98055
425-226-1534
www.scn.org

Community Home Health and Hospice
Longview, WA 98632
800-378-8510
www.chhh.org

Journey Program: Children's Hospital Regional Medical
Center
Seattle, WA 98105-9907
866-987-2000
www.seattlechildrens.org

Kid's Grief Group: Hospice of Kitsap County
Silverdale, WA 98383
360-698-4611
www.hospiceofkitsapcounty.org

Lisa's Kids
Bellingham, WA 98226
360-715-2597

Sound Care Kids
Olympia, WA 98509
360-459-8311
www.providence.org

Stepping Stones: S.W. Washington Medical Center
Vancouver, WA 98663
503-972-3000

The Care Foundation
Oak Harbor, WA 98277
360-279-2352

Cork's Place
Kennewick, WA 99336
509-783-7416
www.tricitieschaplaincy.org

The Good Grief Center
Wenatchee, WA 98801
509-662-6069
www.goodgriefcenter.org

The Healing Center
Seattle, WA 98109
206-261-6855
www.healingcenterseattle.com

WICS WINGS
Seattle, WA 98166
206-241-5650
www.widowedinformation.org

Camp Heartland
Milwaukee, WI 53202
414-272-1118
www.CampHeartland.org

Camp Hope
Stevens Point, WI 54481
715-341-0076
www.camphopeforkids.org

Center for Grieving Children
Appleton, WI 54914
920-731-0555
www.bgclubfoxvalley.org/main.asp?id=21

Children's Hospital of Wisconsin Bereavement Services:
Family Services Dept.
Milwaukee, WI 53201
414-266-3325
www.chw.org

Grief Relief: A Collaborative Initiative of Marian College &
Agnesian HealthCare
Fond du Lac, WI 54935
920 923 8952
www.mariancollege.edu/thanatology

Kyle's Korner
Milwaukee, WI 53228
414-327-1370
www.kyleskorner.com

Margaret Ann's Place
Kenosha, WI 53143
262-656-9656
866-455-HOPE
www.margaretannsplace.org

My Good Mourning Place
Milwaukee, WI 53215
414-643-5678, 414-643-5675
www.mygoodmourningplace.org

St. Luke's Hospital
Milwaukee, WI 53215
414-649-6634

Financial Information After a Sudden Death

American Institute of Certified Public Accountants
Personal Financial Planning Division
212-596-6200
www.cpapfs.org

College Savings Plans Network
529 Tax Advantaged Savings Plan
www.collegesavings.org

Credit Standing
Equifax 800-685-1111 www.equifax.com
Experian 888-397-3742 www.experian.com
TransUnion 800-888-4213 www.transunion.com

Martindale-Hubbell Law Directory; Lawyer Locator
www.martindale.com

National Association of Personal Financial Advisors
Arlington Heights, IL 60004
800-366-2732
www.napfa.org

National Foundation for Credit Counseling
800-338-2227
www.nfcc.org

Social Security Administration
800-772-1213
www.ssa.gov

The National Suicide Prevention Lifeline

1-800-273-TALK

Are you in a suicidal crisis? The National Suicide Prevention Lifeline is a 24-hour, toll-free suicide prevention service that is available to anyone in suicidal crisis. If you need help, please dial 1-800-273-TALK (8255). You will be routed to the closest possible crisis center in your area. With more than 130 crisis centers across the country, they provide immediate assistance to anyone seeking mental health services. Call for yourself, or someone you care about. Your call is free and confidential.

Barbara Rubel is a widely acclaimed national keynote speaker on stress management, compassion fatigue, loss, and resiliency. If you want to book Barbara for your training or conference:

Call: 732-422-0400
Email: griefwork@aol.com
Mail: Griefwork Center, Inc.
                 P.O. Box 5177
                 Kendall Park, NJ 08824
Telephone: 732-422-0400

Visit Barbara's Website: www.griefworkcenter.com